THE ART OF THE
SHORT GAME

THE ART OF THE
SHORT
GAME

• •

Tour-Tested Secrets for Getting Up and Down

Stan Utley
with Matthew Rudy

GOTHAM
BOOKS

GOTHAM BOOKS
Published by Penguin Group (USA) Inc.
375 Hudson Street, New York, New York 10014, U.S.A.
Penguin Group (Canada), 90 Eglinton Avenue East, Suite 700, Toronto, Ontario M4P 2Y3, Canada (a division of Pearson Penguin Canada Inc.); Penguin Books Ltd, 80 Strand, London WC2R ORL, England; Penguin Ireland, 25 St Stephen's Green, Dublin 2, Ireland (a division of Penguin Books Ltd); Penguin Group (Australia), 250 Camberwell Road, Camberwell, Victoria 3124, Australia (a division of Pearson Australia Group Pty Ltd); Penguin Books India Pvt Ltd, 11 Community Centre, Panchsheel Park, New Delhi—110 017, India; Penguin Group (NZ), 67 Apollo Drive, Rosedale, North Shore 0745, Auckland, New Zealand (a division of Pearson New Zealand Ltd.); Penguin Books (South Africa) (Pty) Ltd, 24 Sturdee Avenue, Rosebank, Johannesburg 2196, South Africa

Penguin Books Ltd, Registered Offices: 80 Strand, London WC2R ORL, England

Published by Gotham Books, a division of Penguin Group (USA) Inc.

First printing, June 2007
10 9 8

Gotham Books and the skyscraper logo are trademarks of Penguin Group (USA) Inc.

LIBRARY OF CONGRESS CATALOGING-IN-PUBLICATION DATA

Utley, Stan.
   The art of the short game : tour-tested secrets for getting up and down / Stan Utley; with Matthew Rudy.
      p. cm.
   ISBN 978-1-592-40292-2 (hardcover)
   1. Short game (Golf) I. Rudy, Matthew. II. Title.
   GV979.S54U87 2007
   796.352'3—dc22

2007012044

Printed in the United States of America

Set in Augustal with Rotis Sans Serif

CONTENTS

FOREWORD

by Peter Jacobsen

Jay Haas has been a friend of mine for a long time, and early in 2003 we were paired together at the Buick Invitational in San Diego. Jay was really excited about his game, and had a lot of great things to say about the putting and short-game work he had been doing with Stan Utley.

At that point, I had been headed toward becoming a part-time player on the PGA Tour—both because my outside business interests started taking up a lot more of my time and because I simply wasn't scoring as well as I wanted to. I was hitting the ball as well or better as I ever had, but my pitching, chipping, and putting just weren't competitive. I played twenty-one tournaments in 2002 and made just under $400,000.

Still, the Champions Tour was a year away, so I knew I wanted to keep working on my game. Jay watched me hit it good but struggle for two rounds and miss the cut in San Diego, and he suggested that I give Stan a call. Stan cleared his schedule, and I went over to Scottsdale for a day to hear what he had to say.

I'm really glad I made that trip.

What Stan says about the short game makes sense. It matches what I had been working on in my full swing with my teacher, Jim Hardy, and Stan has a simple, no-nonsense way of getting his points across that clicked with me right away. We made some changes in my putting stroke, but the biggest overhaul came in how I pitched and chipped the ball. I had always made my money on the PGA Tour with my ball-striking skills. After a few hours with Stan, it was if I had a whole new golf game—from 50 yards in.

One of the first things you learn as a tour player is to expect any changes you're making to your swing to take some time to feel comfortable. I was prepared to work at what Stan showed me before I saw results in my scores, but it didn't take long. Within a couple of months, I had back-to-back top-10 finishes at Harbour Town and the Houston Open. But the best was yet to come, in July.

In Hartford, I shot 63 in the first round and led from start to finish, winning my first PGA Tour event since 1995. It's always a thrill to win, but doing it at age forty-nine, when you think your next chance won't be until the Champions Tour, is really special.

Coming down the stretch, I had a one-shot lead and was facing a pitch shot from the rough on the 15th hole. Using the technique Stan taught me, I hit it to three feet and made the putt. It was the shot that won the tournament for me—and one Stan will show you how to hit in Chapter 5.

I joined the seniors in 2004 and was fortunate enough to win the U.S. Senior Open in my first try. My putting, pitching, and chipping is so much more solid now thanks to Stan, and he's actually helping me have to make some tough decisions about how much time to spend playing golf and how much to devote to my off-the-course work.

What does this mean for you? It's simple. Stan knows how to help you get better at the shots you use more than any others during a round of golf. That's the quickest and best way to lower your scores. And he knows how to help you feel confident over the shots that used to make you nervous. I know he did that for me, and I've been playing professionally for more than thirty years now.

So listen to what Stan has to say here. You'll enjoy the game so much more—although the guys you take money from in your regular game might not appreciate it quite as much.

Good luck.

PETER JACOBSEN
Seven-time PGA Tour winner, two-time Champions Tour major winner
Portland, Oregon
September 15, 2006

FOREWORD

by Rob Akins

Years ago, when I first moved to Memphis, I was teaching at a local driving range. As I gave my lessons, I noticed a gentleman sitting on a bench behind me, watching me teach. He never said anything, but he'd come back every few weeks and sit in the same spot. After a few months, I finished my lesson and walked over to him and introduced myself. It was Frank Utley, Stan's father.

Frank Utley told me he worked for the railroad, and he often had eight or ten hours to kill in Memphis before getting back on the train to go back home to Missouri. He had a couple of sons at home—Stan and his brother John—who played golf, and he was really into the game himself. Through Frank, I started teaching John, and pretty soon after that, I met Stan. We hit it off right away, and I've been a teacher and caddie to him, but I've been most fortunate to call him my friend.

What's been amazing for me as a teacher has been to watch Stan do things that are so far above and beyond normal, both as a player and a teacher. As a tour player, Stan was challenged by not being able to hit it very far. He never hit it much more than 245 or 250 off the tee. He had to chip and putt way above average just to compete, and he did that. He played more than ten years on tour, and won the Chattanooga PGA Tour event as well as three Nike Tour events. The pressure was always on Stan's putter and wedges, but he always believed in his talent and that he could get it done that way. I have so much admiration for him and his will to succeed.

Stan's liabilities in terms of power really pushed him to be great with the putter and wedges. He learned how to use his mind, and he showed me how powerful visualization can be in this game.

I had been teaching Stan for several years when we decided that I'd caddie for him at some Nike Tour (now Nationwide Tour) events in the summer of 1995. The week before we were going to get together, I looked in the paper Sunday morning and saw that Stan was in the middle of the pack at the Nike Louisiana Open. The phone rang, and it was Stan. He told me he was shaving, because he wanted to look good in the pictures they took of the tournament winner. Stan had just gone to see a presentation from Tony Robbins and had literally walked over hot coals in a confidence-building exercise. The experience had really made an impression on him. I tried to think of a nice way to point out that he was pretty far behind, but he told me that a hurricane was coming in from the Gulf and he was going to walk on fire.

Stan has always been an incredibly positive person, and a person of deep faith. I kind of wrote off what he was saying that morning as Stan was pumping himself up. I went out fishing with my boys that day and didn't think much more about it. That night, the phone rings again, and it's Stan. He said he was out celebrating (which, for him, was ordering a Grand Slam at Denny's—he's a man of simple tastes). In howling wind, Stan went out and shot 62 to win the tournament by two shots over Keith Fergus. Only a handful of people broke par that day, but Stan said he walked on fire.

Later that year, Stan took some time off when his daughter was born. He told me he was really concerned where he was on the Nike Tour money list, because they didn't give out as many cards for the PGA Tour as they do now. We talked about it, and he decided that he needed to go out and win again to take the pressure off, so he could spend more time at home with his wife and daughter. So Stan went out there and won the Miami Valley event by seven shots. He just decided he wasn't going to miss, and he only missed a few inside twenty feet for the week. He almost didn't worry about speed, because he knew it was going in the hole.

I was caddying for him at another event that summer when he pulled a shot badly into a greenside bunker. Instead of getting upset, he told me that that might be where he was meant to play the next shot from. He holed the bunker shot out. I use that story with the tour players I teach to emphasize how important concentration, calmness, and focus is to playing golf. I learned those lessons from Stan.

Stan's one of the few people I've ever known who could play golf and look like he was never going to miss. For most players, they leave it at that and don't take it to the next level. But Stan went out and absorbed everything he could about the short game and sorted through it, deciding what would help him get even better and what wouldn't. He's always had incredibly strong convictions about his faith and about right and wrong, but you won't find somebody more open to new ideas and willing to listen to what you have to say. That combination of talent and the ability to listen and share is what makes Stan a special, special teacher.

Not only is he going to be able to tell you how to do it, he's done it at the highest level, and he knows what it feels like, and he knows how to help you feel it. The magic of what he's telling you here is not just about technique. It's about teaching you how to see what he sees, and giving you the tools to then execute the shot.

There are a lot of books out there that'll tell you how to build a plane. Stan's gift is that he's going to show you how to fly it.

ROB AKINS
Director of Instruction
Spring Creek Ranch Golf Club
Top 50 instructor
Golf Digest's America's 50 Greatest Teachers

INTRODUCTION

. . . .

There's no doubt it's exciting to watch a guy like Tiger Woods bomb it 315 yards, taking it right over the corner of the dogleg and leaving himself a wedge into the green. I'm in just as much awe as the average guy is when I see him do that, and I've been a tour player myself for more than twenty years.

But the truth is, most players are never going to be able to do what Tiger does with his driver. Heck, there might only be three or four guys on Tour who can do what he does in terms of hitting the ball with power. But watch what Tiger does when he's 30 yards off the green and has a tough pitch to a tight pin. He's an artist on those short shots.

How do I know that?

Because that's how I made my career. I never averaged more than 270 yards off the tee. I was never the best ball-striker on tour. In fact, when Fred Griffin charted my swing down at Grand Cypress, Dr. Ralph Mann, the guy who built the swing model that Fred used, walked by and said I looked like a pretty good 10-handicapper. I had already won on tour by then. I competed out there because of my short-game and putting skills. Now, I make my living teaching other players to use the fundamental skills I was fortunate enough to learn at an early age, and that I relied on so heavily later in my career. With my ball-striking, I never hit more than ten or eleven greens a round. Without a short game, I would have had to find a new line of work.

I set the PGA Tour record for fewest putts for nine holes—six, at the 2002 Air Canada Championship. Everybody thinks that's a putting record, but what it really is, is a short-game record. I missed a bunch of greens, but holed out two bunker shots, made a putt from the fringe and left myself tap-ins on all my other chips.

You might not be able to relate to Tiger Woods hitting the ball 300 yards on the fly, but I can promise you that you can relate to me. I probably hit only ten or eleven greens per round during my PGA Tour career, but I earned money because I could get up and down. If you're a 10- or 15-handicapper, you're hitting between three and seven greens per round. The rest of your score hinges on how well you can negotiate your chips, pitches, and bunker shots.

You can cut a lot more strokes from your score by improving your short game than you can by adding twenty more yards to your tee shot. And you can do it with the coordination and instincts you already have. You need to be strong and flexible (and, preferably, six-foot-two) to bomb it off the tee. To have a good short game, you just have to understand and learn to apply the physics of how it works.

In this book, you'll likely learn an entirely different game than the one you've been playing—or, if you're a little older like I am, maybe even remember some old fundamentals you used to use. From 50 yards and in, you'll have a complete set of fundamental techniques that will give you a much greater arsenal of shots. You'll be able to "see" what kind of shot a certain situation calls for, and have the ability to hit it. Just knowing what shot to play—a low-running shot to a back corner pin, or a lofted shot to a tight one—dramatically improves your chances of getting up and down. Knowing how to practice those kinds of shots so that you can see them and then *execute* them changes you from a 90-shooter to an 85-shooter over a weekend, and to somebody who can break 80 every once in a while before the summer is out. And that's with you hitting your full shots the same way you do now. You'll go from basically chipping and hoping—playing defense or out of fear with your short game—to going on offense and trying to hole some of those shots out with a confident plan.

In fact, I'll bet that as your short game improves, your long game will get better, too. Why? Because you will better understand how the swing works through impact, and the more confident you feel about your short game, the less fear you'll feel standing over your approach shots. Instead of trying to steer away from bunkers, you'll give them the proper respect but not be too concerned if you have to play your way out of them.

The Art of the Short Game is broken down into ten chapters. Chapter 1 will lay out the mind-set you need to have a good short game. I'll show you how I "see" the options in front of me around the green. Chapter 2 covers the fundamentals of short-game shots—and they're the same whether you're hitting a 50-yard pitch or a 20-foot chip. Chapter 3 is devoted to your equipment—finding the perfect lineup of wedges for your bag and your game, and the characteristics each of them needs to have for you to have maximum shot flexibility and consistency. In Chapter 4, I'll take you through the basics of chipping—your bread-and-butter shot. Chapter 5 takes you back from the hole a bit to learn the art of pitching—judging distance, making consistent contact, and getting up and down more often. We'll talk about the art of sand play in Chapter 6—how it's not nearly as hard as you think, and how you can make your ball check and stop, roll out, or land softly, all with a few simple adjustments in your setup. Everyone knows golf isn't usually about perfect lies, so Chapter 7 covers trouble shots—what to do when the ball is way above your feet or buried in the sand. Once you graduate from the basics (which will help you hit 90 percent of the shots you'll face on the course), you can move on to Chapter 8 and try some of the advanced shots I teach tour players. I'll talk about some of the things I've been working on with the tour players I teach—Darren Clarke, Peter Jacobsen, and Jay Haas, among others. You'll see some amazing parallels between what they practice and what applies to your game. I've developed a complete set of drills to help any player get better around the green, and in Chapter 9, I'll show them to you. The last chapter, Chapter 10, offers a quick reference guide to the things we've learned along the way.

It's an awesome feeling to hit it in there tight for birdie when you need to win a match. But I'll bet you'll get almost as much enjoyment out of rolling a tough chip up to tap-in range under pressure to beat your friends. Follow the advice in this book and you'll be doing both soon enough.

Good luck!

CHAPTER 1

HOW TO SAVE YOUR SCORE

· ·

Walking down the practice range at a PGA Tour event is a humbling experience. And that's just as true for an average player as it is for me. When you see the way a guy like Tiger Woods or Ernie Els hits the ball—with so much power and what seems like almost no effort—it's like he's playing a different game.

Actually, those guys *are* playing a different game. Tiger, Ernie, and the longest hitters on the PGA Tour can carry the ball 300 yards with the driver. I don't know about you, but when I play a 450-yard par-4, I'm hitting way more than an 8- or 9-iron into the green. I'm probably hitting a hybrid club, even if I really catch my tee shot. It even sounds different when those guys hit it.

The only problem with admiring those guys is this: You can practice forever, using the best techniques and the best instruction available, and get yourself into the best shape of your life, but 99 percent of you aren't ever going to be able to do what those guys can do. It's like hitting a ninety-eight-mile-per-hour fastball or throwing down a 360-degree dunk. Only a few people were born with the talent to do it. It's why they make the big money and play on television every weekend.

But before you get discouraged, let me tell you where I come in. Some skills that tour players have *are* skills you can learn and apply to your own game. Tiger gets almost as much notoriety for his incredible touch around the green as he does for how far he can hit it. And it's that touch that's the difference between shooting 75 on a bad ball-striking day and scraping out a 71, or turning a smooth 68 into a 65.

I know this first hand, because I didn't make my living as a tour player for more than twenty years because of my ball-striking. I did it on my short game and putting. I've never been a guy who could hit it tremendously far. Even now, with all the modern driver technology available, I'm happy to get it out there 270. But I was always able to save my score by getting up and down when I missed greens (and I missed a lot of them) and birdie-ing the par-5s the old fashioned way, by laying up and hitting a pitch shot in there tight.

I can look back now and understand how I came about my strong short game. First, I was taught great fundamentals. I also had a drive to succeed. Just like the players at your club who always seem to win the big match, I found a way to get it into the hole, despite my lack of strong ball-striking. Players who score understand how to control the flight, trajectory, and spin on short-game shots, and can predict how the ball will react on the ground.

I can definitely relate to the way you play golf. In my PGA Tour career, I probably averaged hitting 10 or 10.5 greens a round. I wasn't a good ball-striker. I had to make my score the same way you do—by saving par and working for my birdie opportunities.

You've heard it before: A good short game is a valuable thing to have. But there is more to it than simply understanding the mechanics of hitting a chip shot or a bunker shot. It's a lot more than just knowing how to hold it and what the motion for those shots looks like. I believe that understanding *how* the club works—for every kind of short shot—gives you so much more flexibility in what shots you play. Once you understand the *how*, you'll start to see possibilities around the green you hadn't even considered before. You'll feel comfortable with your choices, and you'll approach your short game from a whole different perspective. Instead of being anxious and just trying to get the ball on the green somewhere, you're going to hit those shots positively, with the intent to hit them close and, yes, make them.

How do I know this? I've helped a lot of players, from the tour level to complete beginner, transform the way they approach the short game. And when you gain that confidence with your short game, it spreads throughout the rest of your game. You feel more relaxed on the tee and over your approach shot, because you know you've got some margin for error and a comfort level if you miss the green. It also gets a lot more fun playing matches against your buddies. The hardest opponents to face are the guys who are a threat to get it up and down from *everywhere*. You're going to be one of those people. Just make sure to tell your friends to buy their own copies of this book when they ask.

I believe my short-game talent comes from the way I was brought up in the game. I was like lot of other kids growing up in a small town. If there was daylight, I was out there playing something. Baseball, basketball, golf. The part I always loved about golf was that you could go out there by yourself and be totally responsible for what happened or didn't happen. I also loved to figure shots out on my own, with nobody else around— especially short-game shots.

Between my ninth- and tenth-grade years, they changed our little local course, West Plains Country Club, from nine to eighteen holes. One of the par-5s on the old course was converted into a piece of the driving range, but the green from that hole was left as a practice target. I just wore out that green through my high school and college years, hitting thousands and thousands of shots into it—pitch shots, chip shots, you name it. My dad took me to see a man named Ken Lanning—who was famous around my part of Missouri as a player and teacher—to learn the fundamentals. Mr. Lanning gave me the basics, and he sent me to see a guy named Jim Parkin in Poplar Bluff, Missouri, to learn the fundamentals of hitting wedge shots.

Mr. Parkin taught me two fundamental things about the short game—pivoting and compressing the ball on the face of the club—that I've used ever since. And they're two things I'm going to hit again and again in this book. Mr. Parkin gave me a short-game lesson, then sent me back to West Plains to practice what he taught me. I had an old Ben Hogan Special sand wedge, and that thing became my best friend. I'd hit fifty or sixty shots to that green, then go fix my ball marks. I'd pick the balls up and do it again. Every day. By the end of the summer, if I wanted to hit a shot and make it kick to the left, I knew how to do that. If I wanted it to hit, check, and move right, I could do that. By the time the world came out with an L-wedge, when I was in college, I said to myself, what do I need one of those for? I've already got all those shots with my sand wedge. Mr. Parkin taught me how a wedge worked. Armed with that information, I could hit any shot I wanted by putting the club in the right position to make it do what I wanted the ball to do.

To me, golf was always "What did you shoot?" I don't think I fixated on the fact that I didn't hit it as good or swing as pretty as the other players. But I do know that I was well into my college career at the University of Missouri before I realized that not everybody thought it was "normal" to get up and down thirteen times during a round. When you're a little kid—or you can't hit it very far—you can't always get to every green in regulation. As I moved from high school to college and on into professional golf, I did improve as a ball-striker, but because the courses kept getting tougher, I remained dependent on my short game. I always just chipped and putted and did what it took to shoot a score. I've always believed that you shouldn't be thinking about what you can't do, or what you're not supposed to be able to do. You should be relentlessly playing to your strengths. Putting yourself in position to do what you're good at. Taking advantage of the skills you *do* have. I always seemed to have a feel for getting up and down. You too can increase your ability to shoot a score by applying the fundamentals you learn here.

So much of golf instruction these days is about learning how to swing. How to hit full shots on a driving range and look good doing it. There's a place for that, for sure, but the game shouldn't become too much about technique. I actually think this is a problem at the PGA Tour level to a certain degree. I see some younger players out there who have just fantastic golf swings, but they mostly seem to go at it 100 percent on every swing. There's no finesse there, or any sense of feel about what kinds of shots work best in certain situations. Those guys can go low under good conditions, but struggle when they aren't swinging it perfect, or are confronted with something that requires a little creativity. Not to beat a dead horse, but that's why Tiger Woods is killing everybody right now. He's got a good swing, and he has all the shots—in both his long game and short game. And he knows how to scrape it around when he's not swinging good and save his score with his short game.

That's the point of this game, right? Scoring? I hope what I'm going to show you in this book is athletic and natural, and not a connect-the-dots technique. When you try the things in this book, you're going to start out feeling like you're giving up control. You're going to be hitting mini-shots with more speed on the clubhead end than you've ever had before. That's going to be scary for a while, but it'll be liberating in the end. You hear tour players talk about feel and touch. You'll understand what that means, and what that *feels* like, when you finish this book.

I'll never forget what a club pro told me when I was a college player. He told me he had kids lined up on the driving range who hit it better than me. I don't know if he meant that as a compliment or not. But the second part of that story was that all of those kids who hit it so good went out and shot 83. I was consistently breaking par with my swing. My senior year, I was second-team all-American. It's not about what it looks like. It's about what score you write down.

Of course, the same thing that makes the short game accessible for the average player is what makes it so frustrating, too. It's definitely easier to accept hitting a bad shot from 200 yards away from a tough lie in the rough than it is from a perfect lie 10 yards off the green on nice, flat fringe. Even if you aren't very good with your short game, you'll still feel like you missed an opportunity if you stub that chip or blade it over the green.

So much of that frustration comes from the fact that short-game shots are usually hit with a small, controlled swing. You certainly don't have to be physically strong to have a good short game. It feels like something you ought to be able to do without too much practice or effort. But I'm sure you know what it feels like to overcontrol the club. You squeeze the grip so tight because you want to direct it through the grass. The result is some kind of awkward stab at the ball, and you end up moving it only a few feet. You're burning mad, and you probably have to hit another one of the same kind of shots. When you squeeze the life out of the grip like that in an effort to make the club do what you want, you're stealing all of your feel. You're stealing all of your talent.

Take your chipping game. If you've only ever learned how to hit one kind of chip shot—and I'll bet it's the one where you open your stance and play the ball way back—you're going to struggle and get frustrated. First of all, that kind of shot doesn't work very well because of how you're set up. That shot also doesn't work for every circumstance and every different kind of lie. I'm going to teach you how to hit a better basic chip that you can use all over the golf course, plus how to see and hit the other kinds of shots you need to make to lower your scores.

For example, if you have to hit it over a bunker to a pin that doesn't have much green around it, you're going to have to play a shot with some loft. If all you're comfortable doing is hitting a little bump and run shot with your 7-iron, you're pretty much going to have two choices, and neither of them is good. You can hit that little 7-iron shot over to the fat part of the green and try to two-putt, or you can try to hit a lofted shot that you've never practiced and aren't comfortable hitting. The odds are, you'll scuff that one into the bunker and have to hit a bunker shot to a tight pin. If you don't get up and down from there, you've just turned a potential par into a triple bogey. That's how a 10-handicapper turns rounds of 80 into ho-hum 87s.

I'm serious when I say that a day or two of work on what I'm teaching here can transform your short game to the point that you can realistically expect to reduce your handicap five or six shots if you're a 15-handicapper. Almost immediately. The short game is that important to your overall scoring, and the average guy has that much potential to get better in that area. In the average 90-shooter's round, he's putting thirty-six or thirty-seven times, hitting fourteen or fifteen chip shots, eight or nine pitch shots, and three or four greenside bunker shots. Compare that to the eight or nine tee shots with a driver a player might hit in a round and tell me where you can shave the most shots, immediately.

The key to saving your score is understanding the mechanics of short-game shots and actually *seeing* the options available to you. If you know how to hit different shots and you pick the best one for the situation, even a mediocre effort is going to give you pretty good results. The average 18- to 20-handicapper doesn't see the shots I'm talking about here. Once you start breaking 90 regularly, you might see a few more of the possibilities, but you have trouble hitting them consistently. This book will get you to see the possibilities, understand what it takes to hit them, and have the ability to pull them off. I promise you that is well within your ability, no matter what your handicap is right now.

When I teach a short-game lesson here at Grayhawk Golf Club in Scottsdale, I devote the first part of the lesson to watching what you do with your various short-game shots. I want to know what you do, but I also want to hear from you what you *think* you do. As I said in the last paragraph, so many players believe that you need to chip from an open stance, with the ball played back. That way, you can hit with a descending blow. True, you can hit down on it, but chipping that way makes doesn't actually give you the most margin for error. If you're doing that, I want to hear you tell me why, and what kind of consistency you get from it. I'm not going to automatically change your technique if you're consistently getting it up and down that way, but I can promise you that there is a much simpler way to get consistently good results.

So much of what I see in the short game seems to be a player's subconscious telling him to get a pitch or chip up in the air. When you subconsciously try to get the ball in the air, you usually get your body tilting back, away from the target, the shaft of the club tilting back and the hands breaking down and scooping to try to get loft. All of those things are the opposite of what really makes the ball go up in the air.

I saw a 15-handicapper last week who had spent the last *year* trying to improve his short game. He even built a green in his backyard. He worked and worked at it, but all he did was get worse. He didn't realize that he literally dove backwards, away from the target, on every shot. I teach that you set up with your weight and spine tilt to the left, toward the target, and hit the ball by turning and pivoting, not by tilting and scooping. Once I got him feeling what that turn was supposed to be like, he got better in ten minutes. He chipped it better. He hit better pitches. He got better out of the bunker. Just by turning and compressing the ball to make it go up in the air.

You'll come to discover that the short game the way I teach it is more precise than what you're used to. I teach picking a spot on the green to land every shot, and being pretty precise about that. That's more involved than simply hitting and hoping, like a lot of players do. You'll definitely go through cycles where your short game isn't as sharp as it could be. When you go through a spell like that with your putter, your scores will suffer because you simply aren't making putts. The good thing about improving your short game is that when you're off, your average chip might end up four or five feet from the hole instead of three. Your best chip isn't going to get any better—after all, in the hole is in the hole—but your average chip will get way, way better.

Your level of expectation on these shots is certainly going to go way up. When you have a precise idea of what kind of shot you want to hit, and you see the spot you want to play that shot to, you're going to have a whole different kind of focus in your short game. It's like having a straight, uphill three-footer that you know you can three-putt and still win. There's a feeling of confidence that comes with standing over a shot you know you can handle—one you can go on offense with and try to make, as a opposed to being on defense.

When I'm looking at a short-game shot, if I can get my club on the back of the ball, I'm thinking about trying to make it. That's called being on offense. I'm realistic about the fact that

I'm not going hole every chip, but I believe I can, and that helps me make my fair share. On a basic bunker shot, I'm planning to make it, and less than satisfied if I'm more than three feet away. On a 50-yard pitch, I'm expecting my ball to hunt the hole and end up inside eight feet. Now, you're going to have your own level of expectation on your short-game shots, but there's no reason why you can't go from a D to a B+ or an A−. Right away.

What I have to share is, in my opinion, the easiest way to hit short-game shots. It might be difficult for you to unlearn and replace what you already do at first. But what I want to emphasize is that it doesn't take an extreme amount of talent or coordination to do this. It's in line with what a teacher would tell you about your full swing. It's about being on plane and swinging in an around motion. We're giving the swing energy and balance by using hips and knees to pivot around the shot, and we're using the hands and arms to control the face through impact. It's an easy method. You don't have to be a tour player to do it. I've taught people of every age and strength level to do this. I've helped fourteen-year-old AJGA girls' tournament champions hit the same shots that big, strong Darren Clarke hits.

Let me tell you a little bit about how I think you should use this book. The best part about the basics I learned from Mr. Parkin is that they apply to almost every shot I talk about here. Even if all you do is work on your grip and get a sense for how the bounce on your clubs should work, you're going to get better. So start with the information in the next chapter—the basics that apply to hitting chips, pitches, and bunker shots. Go out to the practice range—or even your backyard—with a little bucket of balls and fool around with the basics. Get a feel for how to control the loft of your club at impact and you're on your way to lower scores. You might blade a few here and there, but you're going to hit some of the most solid chip shots you've ever hit. Once you get the feeling of compressing the ball—maybe even for the first time—your eyes will open. It'll be like, man, this is how it's *supposed* to be.

Once you have the basics of grip, posture and weight distribution down, use Chapter 2 to make sure you've got the right equipment in your bag for the job. Then you can get serious with each different kind of short-game shot. You can work your way through the chipping chapter, Chapter 4. The chip swing is the smallest one, and it's the basis for the larger pitching swing I'm going to talk about in Chapter 5. And, in reality, a chipping swing is really the bottom of a good full swing, like you'd use on, say, a 7-iron. What you'll learn from the chipping chapter is what good club-turf contact feels like—making a descending blow while reducing the loft of the clubhead, instead of adding it by scooping. Once you start making that turf contact, you'll be surprised about how quickly you can dial in your distance control. You're awakening instincts and athleticism that are already there.

When you work your way up to pitch shots, you'll be developing the skill of using the bounce on the bottom of the club. You'll be using more of the true loft on the club to hit higher shots, and adding a little more wrist hinge, arm swing, and pivot to the chipping swing you already learned. I've heard a lot of players complain about middle-length pitch shots. For some reason, they think that 40- or 50-yarders are harder to judge when it comes to distance, compared to making a full swing. I've never found that to be true, either for myself or for players I teach. Anytime you get a chance to get closer to the hole, I think you have a better chance to hit that shot closer than one from 100 or 120 yards. You can see your target better. You can see the contour of the greens better. And if you've developed the sense for the bounce on the bottom of the club, you'll find that it's relatively easy to dial in your distance to at least within 10 feet from 40 yards. I don't know what kind of short game you have now, but I'm betting that if you could regularly put your 40-yard pitch shots 10 feet from the hole, with an occasional one knocked stiff, you'd be happy.

Understanding how to use the bounce on your club naturally extends from hitting pitch shots to the bunker—where the shots you hit are pretty much *all* about using bounce. Once you learn how to get the bounce skipping through the sand the way it should and positioning yourself so that you can deliver the club-head consistently in the same spot, you're going to start to get the same feel tour players do out of the bunker—that it's like cheating. It's just not a hard shot, once you get the feel for good fundamentals. Work on the basics I'll talk about in Chapter 6 and spend about thirty minutes on the bunker drills I'm going to describe in Chapter 9, and you'll be hitting confident sand shots in time for next Saturday's round. If you don't have to worry about being dead if you hit it in the bunker, imagine how much stress that will take off your approach game.

You might be wondering if tour players face the same problems you do with the short game. Absolutely. It's a matter of degree, of course—Darren Clarke isn't laying sod over his chip shots, but he definitely wants them to get better. In Chapter 8, I'll show you what I work on with the tour players I teach, and how what they work on is similar to what you need to work on. I'll also show you some expert techniques—like a super-high flop shot—that might come in handy once you've graduated from hitting the basic chip, pitch, and bunker shots.

I know some of this sounds almost too good to be true. You're probably thinking to yourself, it's easy for him to sit here and make all kinds of promises about holing out shots from all over the golf course. But I've enjoyed working with players of all skill levels and athletic ability over the last few years. Overwhelmingly, the feedback I get at the end of the session is this: "I never knew it was this easy," or "I wish I had known this years ago." We're playing an individual game. I'm not here to say there's one way to do anything, but the people who have applied these fundamentals have gone away with big smiles on their faces.

I'm not working any magic here. I'm just showing you what I think is an easier way to get the job done. My talent seems to be being able to describe how to do that in a pretty straightforward way. Let's get started.

CHAPTER 2
THE BASICS

. . . .

A half dozen times a year, I speak to large groups about short-game and putting basics. And when I give my talk about the things I teach in chipping and putting, I get most of my confused looks when I talk about how those parts of your game really aren't any different than your full swing, at least in terms of fundamentals.

But wait. You've always been taught a different setup for your chip shots, right? I know that when I ask most average weekend players to show me what they do to hit a chip shot, they do the same thing: Turn to an open stance and play the ball way back. As you've heard me say in both *The Art of Putting* and here already, I don't think there's any reason to make any shot harder than it has to be. Taking the club outside the target line and chopping down on it with a 7-iron can work, if you practice a lot and usually have decent lies. But why would you want to do it that way when there's an easier way—a way that you can learn in a weekend?

One thing you'll learn right away from me is that with the exception of a few high-loft specialty shots, the basics of hitting a chip or a pitch shot aren't any different than what you'd use for a full swing. In other words, you can apply what you already do— and what your full-swing teacher is probably already telling you—to your short game. I simply don't believe the short game is some separate and distinct cousin to the full swing. I play every shot around the green with my normal grip. As I get closer to the green, my stance gets narrower—from the same as a middle-iron shot on a full pitch to where my heels are about four inches apart. Like I said, I'm not coming up with anything new for these shots.

I put my hands on the club with the grip down in my fingers, not across my palms—which is a common mistake I see a lot of players make, on both full-swing and short-game shots. If you get the club up in your palms, it restricts the swing of the club-head. It doesn't let you hinge and unhinge the club properly. You also have more feel in your fingertips than you do in your palms, and I'm interested in getting the most sensitive part of

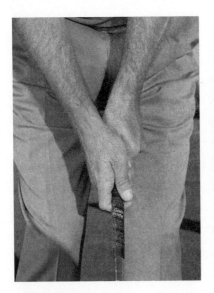 

(ABOVE LEFT) I use this grip for all of my short-game shots. It's neutral, meaning that the creases created by my thumbs and the sides of my hands are parallel to each other and point up toward my right collarbone.

(ABOVE RIGHT) I use an overlapping grip, and I make sure to hold the handle in my fingers, not down in my palms.

  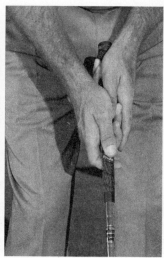

(ABOVE LEFT) Because my grip is in my fingers, the shaft hangs below the angle of my forearms. This promotes a good wrist hinge.

(ABOVE CENTER) Notice how the fingertips of my right hand make good contact with the grip. This is a key component of feel.

(ABOVE RIGHT) Compare the short-game grip with my putting grip. To putt, I use a reverse overlap, with the grip running up the lifelines of both hands, versus down in the fingers. This grip is designed to get the shaft running up the forearm plane.

your hands on the club as much as possible, because your feel for distance is going to be better. The club should run along the crease that is created by the top of your palm and the bottom of the first knuckles of your fingers. The grip is running parallel to the top of your palm, not diagonally across the palm, which is how I'd tell you to hold your putter. Because your wrists don't hinge on a putt, the shaft of your putter should run in line with your forearms. On shots that require a wrist hinge—which is basically every shot besides a putt—the club points below the line of your forearms.

You're probably already familiar with the concept of weak, neutral, and strong grips. Let me tell you what my definition of those terms are so that we don't get confused. If you set your grip in front of you and hold it up in front of your chest, the V's created by the sides of your hands and your thumbs will point to your right collarbone in a neutral grip. In a weak grip, the V's point almost straight up, toward your chin. In a strong grip, the V's turn more to the right, so that they're aimed at your right shoulder. (Remember to reverse all of these directions if you're a left-hander.) You can also have your hands independently turned to different degrees of weak and strong. For example, if you turned your left hand out toward the target and your right out away from the target, your left hand would be set up really weak, and your right would be really strong.

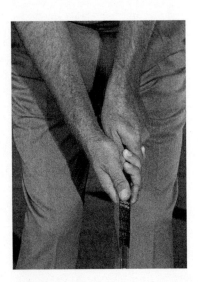 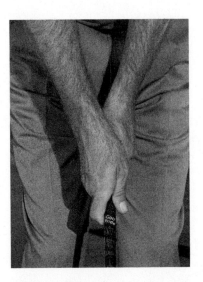

(ABOVE LEFT) In a strong grip, the creases created by my thumbs and the sides of my hands point away from the ball, toward my right shoulder. With this grip, you'll use less forearm rotation to play low shots.

(ABOVE RIGHT) In a weak grip, the creases point toward my chin. It's hard to rotate the forearms correctly with this grip, and you'll tend to hit higher shots.

I like to see a grip that's more neutral than anything else. My right hand is in a neutral position, while my left hand is a touch strong. One of the key elements of what I teach in the short game is how to use your forearm rotation to create different shots—rotating to de-loft the face of the club for a low shot and holding the forearms off to hit a high shot. I believe that when you start with a neutral grip, you have all of those shots available to you just by making a relatively simple adjustment in your forearm rotation. If you use a weak grip, you will need a lot of forearm rotation to lower your ball flight. Your misses will likely come from scooping the ball at impact. Whatever you do, you want to avoid a grip that's too weak. If you set up with a grip that's too strong, essentially you're starting out with the forearms already rotated. If you rotate any more, you're going to hit the ball low and left. A strong grip requires little forearm rotation. You'll be good at the low shots and struggle to hit high, soft ones.

If a person has a good grip, and the club is straight in front of him, he should be able to hinge the club up and down in front of him, and the leading edge should move straight up and down. If you hinge that club up and down and the toe of the club leans left of the heel, then your grip is too strong. If it leans to the right, then your grip would be too weak.

If you set up with a strong grip, this is what happens to the clubface when you rotate your forearms through impact—it shuts down, and you hit the shot left.

Does that mean you can't hit great shots with a strong grip? Of course not. Paul Azinger is one of the greatest short-game artists of all time, and he's been phenomenal with a strong grip. But Paul uses a different technique than I do. He's awesome at hitting his short-game shots without rolling his arms. To hit a chip shot, he takes loft off his wedge by bowing his wrists rather than rotating his forearms, like I teach. Paul plays to his strengths. He has always played more low shots. If you have a strong grip like Paul, you have to recognize that you'll close the clubface on the backswing. This reduces loft and eliminates the club's bounce. Starting from a more fundamental grip will speed up your ability to learn different shots around the green.

I need to make an important point about your short-game grip: Pay regular attention to it. Personally, when I was playing full time, I hit hundreds and hundreds of pitches and chips every week, as do the tour players I teach. I know my fundamentals—even my grip—can drift on occasion. Since the grip is your connection to the club, it can play a big role in your consistency—or lack of it—without you noticing any problem. I make almost a dozen trips a year to tour events around the world to give the guys I teach "checkups," and a lot of the time, we solve most of the problems right away with simple adjustments in fundamentals that have drifted a little bit out of place. The grip is the easiest one to lose track of, especially if you've made a recent change. Be sure to keep watch on it.

When it comes to short-game stance and posture, I want you to feel like what you're doing in your short game is related to your full-swing setup, not something completely foreign and different. After all, I believe you should be making a real pivot in these swings—smaller than you'd make for a full shot, but still a noticeable pivot—so you should feel athletic.

If you don't do anything to change your short-game setup, trust me on this one thing: Tension and stiffness is a feel killer.

Feel is what lets you make sensitive, subtle judgments about how hard to hit a shot and make it go a certain distance. However you set up to the ball, if you get yourself into a rigid, stiff position, with your arms locked or the muscles in your legs tensed up, you're never going to have a good short game. Watch any athlete performing a "touch" maneuver—a basketball player shooting a free throw, a baseball player turning the double play at second base, a quarterback lofting a pass perfectly into a receiver's hands in the back corner of the end zone—and you won't see anything stiff or mechanical. All those moves are fluid and graceful. I want you to develop that same sense of fluidity and feel in your short game.

For greenside shots, I narrow my stance, which makes it easy to rotate my lower body instead of rocking or swaying. As you'll read about in the chapters on chipping and pitching, I don't want you to feel like your lower body is encased in concrete. You need to make a pivot (not a sway) and a narrower stance helps that. What's the difference between a pivot and a sway? A sway is when the hips slide straight back away from the target, as if you were trying to avoid getting tagged in touch football. In a pivot, the hips *turn* instead of shift back, as they would if you were tossing something underhanded. If you look at the way the knees move, you can see the clear difference: In a sway, the knees stay in the same position relative to each other, but both move back, away from the target, and then back toward it. In a pivot, the right knee moves away from the target line, while the left moves toward it. If you picture a long metal bar superimposed over your spine and anchored in the ground, you pivot *around* the fixed bar. In a sway, the bar itself moves back and forth.

In terms of aiming my body, I set up square to the target line or even slightly closed to it with my feet. In other words, if you held a shaft on my shoulders and another one on my hips, both shafts would point parallel to the target line (the line between the ball and where I want the ball to go), or slightly to the right of it. Many, many players are taught to set up open with the shoulders, hips, or both (so that the shafts would point to the left of the target). I don't know why you would want to compensate for where your body is aiming. I want to aim everything down the line I want my ball to travel on. I flare my toes out slightly to allow my hips more mobility, but I still keep my feet aligned square or slightly closed to the target line. The one thing to watch for when you flare your feet out is that you don't let it distort your sense of ball position. We'll cover more of this in chapters 4 and 5.

One principle you're going to hear over and over again when I talk about chipping, pitching, and bunker play is that you need to keep your weight and spine tilt left throughout the swing. On most of my short shots, my weight starts out 65 to 70 percent on my left side, and that balance doesn't change throughout the swing. If you get your weight favoring the left like that, I'll bet you're going to tell me it feels like 90 percent of your weight is left. But that's only because so many players are taught to tilt back away from the target at address to get the ball up in the air.

That tilt to the right is by far the most common mistake I see in the setup, and it has the most damaging consequences. With your right shoulder lower than your left, it *feels* like you get more loft on your shots, but it really just makes it easier for you to blade it or dig the club into the ground a couple inches behind the ball, especially if you're making common mistake number two, which is playing the ball too far back in the stance. People have been taught to make a descending blow on the ball, so it would seem that moving it back in the stance would help you hit it with a descending blow. True, but that's really doing it the hard way, and making it very difficult to make consistent contact. If you play the ball in the middle of your stance with your weight favoring your *left* instead of your right side, your club will be making contact with the ground at the lowest portion of the swing, versus coming in too steep.

I'm not in favor of taking an open stance to hit your chip or pitch shots, because it encourages you take the club back outside the target line, away from your body. The only way to hit a good shot from there is to scoop with your hands or block it toward the target. I think people have been told it's easier to turn through and be in a good impact position if you set up open. I understand those thoughts. But my short shots don't require a lot of follow-through. My club is done two to three feet past the ball. I want to set up so that it's extremely easy to reach my backswing position, so I'm in a good position to start down. Just like putting, my backswing varies depending on how far I want to hit the shot, but my follow-through stays pretty similar, unless I need to hit a real high shot. By setting up square, it's much easier to get the club into an on-plane position in the backswing, so all I have to do is pivot through.

I see so many players set up with the right shoulder low, the ball too far back and the stance open and aimed to the left. I'll even see some players get the ball too far forward in the stance, but it happens without them even knowing it. You can see this if you set up a shot with your left foot very open to the target line. Turn your foot back to square without moving your heel and you'll see what I mean. The ball will usually be an inch or two in front of your left foot (toward the target), way out in front, and in a difficult spot to hit consistently with good contact. My left toe might be slightly open when I set up to a shot, but my toe line—the imaginary line you draw in front of your feet—is definitely parallel to the target line or pointing slightly to the right of it.

Another common mistake is starting with the shaft leaning too far forward—toward the target. That usually happens because of a combination of other mistakes. If your ball position is too far back and your stance is open, you pretty much have to have your hands forward to be able to hit the ball without crashing the club into the ground six inches behind the ball. The concept of de-lofting the club is good—it helps you play shots hitting the ball first, which is required for hitting low shots, as opposed to the ground. But to me, it puts the player in the opposite position to the one I like.

Let me go into some detail to explain what I mean. Your golf swing happens on a plane. If you looked at it from behind, so you were looking toward the target, you could draw an angled line on the shaft of your club that would represent a plane. I basically try to swing my club in a circle and have the shaft remain on this angled line, or plane. As the club swings on the plane, it has two elements. One, it goes around, and the other, it goes up and down. If the around and up and down happen at the same pace, the shaft stays on-plane. The way I move the club with my hands, wrists, and arms affects the plane. Also, I can change the plane with the tilt of my spine, both up and down and side to side.

Leaning your body and tilting to the left creates more of an up-and-down move in the swing, while leaning to the right creates more of an around move. When you pick up the clubhead with your hands and wrists early in the backswing, you create a lot of up and down. If you make a backswing by allowing the arms to rotate around the body with little wrist hinge, you create a more "around" swing. Most poor chippers and pitchers use the wrong combination of these elements. They lean the spine to the right (back away from the target) at address. This creates an around move, and they use their hands and wrists to lift the club on the backswing. They often tilt back more on the downswing and then have to use the wrists to bring the club down sharply back to the ball. This is why they hit it fat and thin.

I teach my students to tilt their spine slightly toward the target at address and ask them to maintain that tilt through the swing. Leaning left helps you maintain the bottom of your swing in the same place all the time, without any need for manipulating the club with your hands. Swinging the club more around with your arms while tilting this way lets the clubhead swing along the ground longer, giving you more room to hit the ball and still make solid contact and come up with a reasonable shot.

When you start out with the shaft leaning forward and the ball back, you pretty much have to chop down on the ball to hit the shot successfully. There are situations where chopping straight down on it is a good play—like when you have to blast the ball from some kind of divot. But for the most part, I think using that kind of technique for every chip leaves very little room for error. If you don't hit the ball first, you're going to skull it or stick the club in the ground. But by bringing the club in more shallow, you have more room to make a mistake without it turning into a horrible shot.

Before we get too carried away here (and before we get to the chapters that deal more specifically with each shot), let me tell you about how I define the different kinds of shots you hit around the green.

You might hear a golf announcer talk about a chip shot or a pitch shot a player is facing, and either the difference between those shots isn't clear or else the announcer is using the terms interchangeably. Some people believe that the difference between a chip and a pitch has to do with how far away from the hole the shot is played from—a chip being something 5 or 10 yards off the green, and a pitch something from a longer distance. Other people believe that a chip rolls more than it flies, while a pitch flies more than it rolls.

For me, the distinction is a lot simpler. In a chip shot, you're reducing the loft of the club through impact and hitting the ball first, and then the ground with the leading edge of the club. In a pitch shot, you're playing the shaft in a more neutral position and hitting the ground with the bounce on the bottom of the club, and then the ball. That's it. The difference is in the kind of impact you create. It doesn't have anything to do with distance. You can hit a long chip shot that's longer than a short pitch, and vice versa. And the flying-versus-rolling description doesn't really work, either, because of the variety of the different green conditions you face. You might have to bump a chip shot into the face of a hill and have it just trickle up to the flag, and you might hit a long pitch to a flag that's below you, so it runs out more.

But in reality, the distinction is academic, because what I'm going to teach you for both kinds of shots is pretty similar. The only changes are what you do with your left wrist. The left wrist is what really controls the clubface, and therefore the shot. You're maintaining a consistent setup and making a shallow swing. That leads to consistent impact. Learning how to vary the shot comes from understanding how the left wrist works. We're going to talk about those differences in the left wrist, and how you can use them to pick the perfect shot for each situation.

Aside from the differences in the left-wrist position, my body moves the same way for both shots. I pivot back with my knees and hips as I set the club with my wrists and right elbow. When I turn through the ball, I lead with my lower-body pivot. What I'm doing is starting with my lower-body pivot, and everything above my waist follows along behind. It's a chain reaction all the way to my shoulders. I want my shoulders and club lagging so that they come to impact from the inside of the target line (or in other words, down the swing plane).

The first time I explain this to people, they often make the mistake of simply pivoting their upper body from the top of the backswing. The lower body stays really passive. If you do that— just turn your shoulders back and through, without any lower-body pivot—you're going to come around over the top and hit from the outside of the target line. It's the same flaw a lot of players have in the full swing. They've never felt how you lead the lower body and lag the upper body. At impact, my thighs and hips are slightly open to the target, but my shoulders are square. I don't want my shoulders way open at impact, which they would be if I was just turning back and forth with my upper body.

Once you get the feel for activating your lower body back and through, some exciting things will start to happen. First, the chain reaction of your lower body working with your lagging upper body will help you hit the ball much farther with much less effort and arm swing. Your impact condition—how "pure" and cleanly you hit the ball—will improve dramatically, and when you start to sense that the ball is going a consistent distance with a given amount of effort, you're going to get really good, really fast, at judging how hard to hit a chip or a pitch. And that's without any real conscious effort to "read" distance. Players ask me all the time how I know how to hit a pitch shot 15 yards as opposed to 19 yards. It's a feel, not some kind of calculation. Once your impact starts getting clean time after time, you'll know how hard *you* need to swing to hit it 15 yards. Do you think about how hard to toss a ball of paper into a trash can? Or how much force you need to use to lift a glass of water? Your brain is pretty smart, and it's wired to figure these things out automatically. You just have to let it. Consistent and efficient mechanics make that much easier to do.

One other piece of the short-game puzzle is the same for every shot you hit—and it's just as important as the mechanics we've been talking about. It's your strategy. It's *how* you think of the shot you're going to hit, not just how you execute it. It's easy to make fun of "visualization" or any of those other fuzzy words teachers like to talk about. But I'm here to tell you that you can get significantly better with your short game by having a consistent process you use for every shot. Even if you don't hit your shots particularly well, you'll have a better sense for what's about to happen and how to prepare for it.

I've had conversations with hundreds of amateur players about what they're thinking before they hit a short-game shot. I wish I could say that most of them were actually thinking the *wrong* thing. It would mean that they had some kind of decision-making process that they were using, even if it was one I didn't really love. But most average players are standing up there without thinking about much at all. Usually, it's some version of "I hope I can just get up there on the green somewhere." I'm not a big fan of being obsessed with mechanics when you're standing over a real shot during a real round of golf, but even thinking about mechanics would be more productive and positive than thinking "I just hope I can get it up there somewhere."

Without going into the actual mechanical preparation steps I take before every shot just yet, let me tell you about how I *think* about each short-game shot I hit. The first thing I do when I walk up to the ball near the green is to run a checklist of all the possibilities that the lie and the shot give me. Can I hit it high or low? Do I have to carry some kind of trouble in front of me, or some kind of tier on the green? How is my ball going to behave when it hits the green? Once I've got an idea of the options, I pick the one that I think is the best choice for the situation. Now, this is where the train goes off the tracks for a lot of players. You need to feel *comfortable* with the choice you make. Just because a situation dictates some kind of high flop shot, if you need to make a bogey to win your hole and you're more comfortable hitting a lower-running chip to 10 feet from the hole, you should be picking the shot that makes you comfortable.

Once I pick my shot, I get totally into hitting that particular shot. I know that's easy for me to say, but there's really no other way to put it. You have to put the decision-making process behind you, stop second-guessing at that point, and feel confident about the shot you're going to hit. Once you read the next few chapters on how to hit those shots, this is going to be easier to do, trust me.

When I'm making two or three brisk practice swings, I'm doing two things. First, I'm visualizing the actual flight of the shot I'm about to hit. If it's a chip shot, I'm picturing the ball hitting and rolling right up to the hole. If it's pitch, I'm watching it fly up on the green and roll out, too. I'm also equating what I'm visualizing with the practice swings I'm making, to help me get a feel for how hard I want to swing on my real shot. Before I implemented a purposeful pre-shot routine, I know I used to leave this step out some of the time. Getting a picture of what you want to do in your head before you try to do it is one of the most effective ways I've found of focusing before hitting a shot.

Once I make my practice swings and visualize the shot, I move right in and hit it, without fooling around or freezing over it. When you take extra time between your practice swings and hitting the real shot, only bad things can happen. First, if you're under pressure at all, that anxiety just builds and makes it less likely that you're going to execute your mechanics smoothly. On an even more basic level, the longer you take between your practice swings and visualization and the actual swing itself, the more separation you get between your feel and your actual swing. As I've said time and time again, your brain is really smart, and it wants to help you. If you go through the trouble to visualize the shot you're trying to hit, don't waste that effort by "forgetting" the visualization by spending a lot of time fidgeting around (or freezing) over the ball before you pull the trigger. I'm a big believer in the idea that your athletic instincts are good ones, and you should trust them.

Of course, it helps to have the right clubs—and the right mechanics—to go with those athletic instincts we all have. Let's get those things in order now.

CHAPTER 3

FINDING THE RIGHT EQUIPMENT

· ·

When you come to see me for a lesson in Scottsdale, you're bringing two things with you—your short game and your equipment. So I always do two things right at the beginning of our time together. The first we already talked about in the last chapter—I'd watch you to see what kind of short-game technique you were using. After that, I'd look in your bag and see what kind of wedges you carry.

It's not so much a matter of what brand of clubs you have, although I sure enjoy my Vokey spin-milled models. In reality, as long as the grooves are in good condition and have specs that match the shots you want to play, they'll work just fine. What I'm looking for are the playing characteristics of your short-game clubs. How many wedges do you have? What lofts and lie angles are they? Do they have a lot of bounce? Not so much bounce? How do they suit what you're trying to do with your chipping, pitching, and sand game? Will they fit the kind of short game I teach? There's no reason to make this harder than it has to be by using tools that don't fit the job.

What I see with most average players—even ones who play a lot of golf—is that they spend way, way more time tinkering on the practice green picking a putter than they do putting together a combination of wedges. How many times have you grabbed your buddy's putter to roll a few with it, to see if he might be on to something? But I'll bet you've never grabbed his sand wedge and hit some chip shots.

I can certainly understand why putters seem to get all the attention. I've been very attached to the putters I've used in my career, to the point that I've only used four different ones over more than twenty years of playing on tour. The putter is the most personal club in the bag. You use it more than any other club, and you *should* spend a lot of time finding one that fits you, looks good, and feels good. But what I'm trying to say is that I'm just as particular about my wedges as I am about my putter. You should be, too. They're going to be as valuable to you as your putter when it comes to saving shots.

I strongly believe you shouldn't ignore your wedges, or be satisfied with the ones that came with the set of irons you bought. Picking wedges that fit you, have the right playing characteristics, and cover a variety of different situations around the green makes you a much, much more complete player. It makes it easier for you to create shots, and it's a cheap way to shave four or five shots off your handicap instantly.

Three factors make up the most important pieces of the puzzle for each wedge in your bag—loft, bounce, and lie angle. The combination of those three things is what makes one wedge feel great in your hands—like you could get up and down from anywhere—and another one feel just *off*. Let's take a look at these factors one at a time:

- **Loft:** Like any other club in your bag (including the putter), wedges come in a variety of lofts. A standard pitching wedge has 48 degrees of loft, a gap wedge has 52 to 56 degrees, and a lob wedge has 60. The higher the loft a club has, the higher (and shorter) you will hit that club. You can get a wedge with any degree of loft between 48 and 60 degrees, and you can even find a few stray 62- or 64-degree wedges out there.

- **Bounce:** If you look at the bottom of your sand wedge, you'll see some extra metal tilting down and away from the leading edge of the front of the clubface. The bottom of the club is shaped differently to help it glide through the turf or sand without digging in too deeply. Think of skipping a rock across a lake. When you skip the rock, you have to throw it so that the trailing edge of the rock hits first. The trailing edge of a sand wedge is the bounce, striking the turf or sand first so that the club skips instead of digging in. A standard sand wedge might have 10 to 12 degrees of bounce, while a lofted wedge like a 60-degree might have four to six degrees of bounce.

- **Lie angle:** Lie angle is the angle at which the shaft comes out of the clubhead. If you set up with your wedge in a natural position and the heel of the club is off the ground, the club has a lie angle that's too flat. If the toe is off the ground, the lie angle is too upright. When you play shots with the entire bottom of your wedge against the turf or sand, you will be taking full advantage of your equipment.

You need to know how these factors fit together so that you can get the most out of the collection of wedges in your bag. Let's start with loft. Tour players usually go with a configuration of three or four wedges. The three-wedge configuration includes a pitching wedge (48 degrees), sand wedge (56), and lob wedge (60 degrees). The four-wedge configuration breaks up the gap between the pitching wedge and sand wedge with, appropriately enough, a gap wedge (52 degrees). I don't think it's necessary to have a 60-degree wedge in the bag, because if you follow

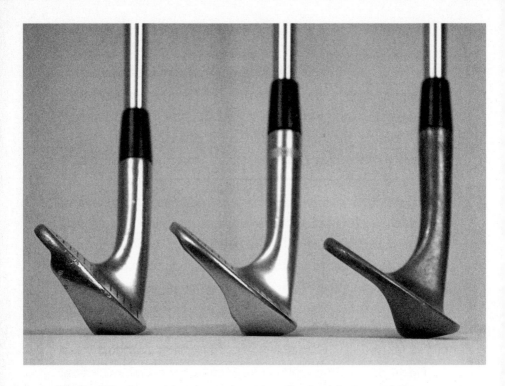

Here are the three wedges I carry in my bag. On the right is my 58-degree wedge, which I use for most short-game shots. In the middle is my gap wedge, which has 53 degrees of loft (bent from 52). On the left is my pitching wedge, which I mostly use for full shots from the fairway. It has 48 degrees of loft.

the basics I'll talk about in the pitching and chipping chapters, you'll be able to add loft with your technique as needed. I carry a pitching wedge, a 53-degree gap wedge (a 52-degree club bent to 53), and a 58-degree wedge that I use for almost all of my chips and pitches.

When it comes to bounce, I'm strongly in favor of using as much of it as you can get away with under the conditions of your golf course. My 58-degree club has 12 degrees of bounce, which makes it skip very easily through the turf or sand instead of digging in. I've heard some teachers say that a club with that much bounce is hard to hit from the fairway because the bounce kicks the club up off the turf. I don't think that's true at all. I've tried hitting pitch shots from the parking lot here at Grayhawk, and the 12 degrees of bounce on my club didn't keep me from hitting it off pavement just fine. I'm guessing concrete is a little firmer than the fairways at your place. More bounce is really going to help you if you play anywhere the turf is soft or sandy—like in the Middle Atlantic or the Northwest. About the only place I can think of that would make me consider trading out for a club with (slightly) less bounce is a really dried out British Open venue. Last year at Royal Liverpool, guys were hitting shots that raised huge clouds of dust instead of divots.

You've probably heard something about lie angle as it pertains to your regular irons. Depending on how tall you are, and how long your arms are, your clubs are built with standard, upright, or flat lie angles. If you have more distance between the tips of your fingers and the ground (either as a taller person or a person with shorter arms), you generally need a club that is built more upright. If you are shorter or have longer arms, you generally need a club that is more flat than standard. You can also have the lie angles of your clubs tailored to compensate for how you hit the ball. A club with an upright lie angle will tend to straighten out a slice, while a club with a flat lie angle will help a person who tends to hit hooks. All of that is just as true for wedges. And since these are your scoring clubs—clubs you're going to come to expect to hit close to the hole regularly—swinging ones with lie angles that aren't right is going to make things more difficult than they have to be.

One thing I've often noticed when I look in players' bags at the clinics I do is that the clubs that come in off-the-rack sets just aren't set up correctly. It's even true for clubs that have been "fitted." Most manufacturers have a standard lie-loft chart that

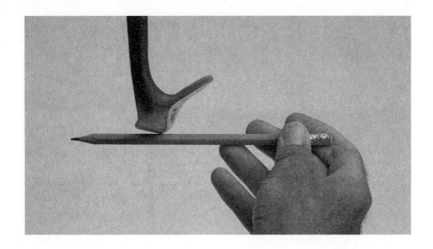

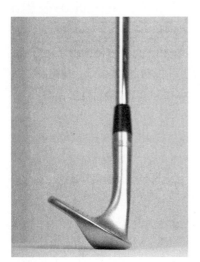

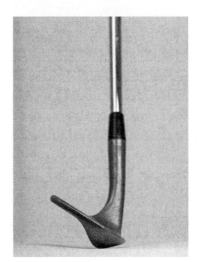

(TOP) Bounce is the angle of the sole of the club that hangs below the leading edge of the wedge. This club has 12 degrees of bounce, which means that angle created by the club and my pencil is 12 degrees. A club with less bounce would sit flatter on the pencil.

(BOTTOM LEFT) Notice how flat this 60-degree wedge with four degrees of bounce sits on the ground compared to the 58-degree wedge with 12 degrees of bounce.

(BOTTOM RIGHT) My 58-degree club is great for virtually any short-game shot. I also hit it about 85 yards from the fairway.

....

dictates how a set of clubs is put together. In my set of clubs, my long irons (3-iron and 4-iron) are built more upright than standard. My middle irons (5-6-7) are neutral, and my short irons (8 through sand wedge) are built with flat lie angles. I don't want to miss my long irons to the right, and I don't want to miss my short irons to the left. Most players end up with clubs that are too upright, usually because the fitter sees that they're a slicer and wants to try to give them some help—which is okay with a 5-iron, but is going to hurt you when you go to hit your wedge.

Even when you buy premium wedges separate from your set, like Titleist Vokeys or Cleveland 588s, you can still come out with wedges that are too upright. Most of the wedges I've measured—even at the tour level—are set up a little bit too upright. Luckily, it's really easy to have a clubfitter bend the club a touch flatter for you. I have a lie-loft machine at the Kostis Mc-Cord Learning Center at Grayhawk, and I can get a player's wedge adjusted just right in less than five minutes. A Titleist Vokey 58-degree wedge comes off the rack with about 64 degrees of lie angle. I like mine to be 62 degrees, because my body type requires a flatter swing. You might need one that's a touch flatter or more upright than that because of your build, but overall, I think pretty much every player needs to be using something a little flatter in their wedges than in the rest of the set.

The problem with wedges that are too upright is twofold. First, the upright lie reduces the effective loft of the club, making you hit it lower, longer, and left. Second, the shorter shaft in the wedge makes it particularly hard to set up with the sole flat on the ground if it's built too upright. You end up with toe off the ground, and you run the risk of digging the heel in and flipping the club over on full shots and making inconsistent contact on your chips and pitches. When the grass catches the heel of the club first (as often happens in deep rough), the heel slows down, while the toe end keeps moving and turns over. That's not good, as you can imagine.

The most valuable club in my bag is my 58-degree wedge. I use a Titleist Vokey wedge with 12 degrees of bounce. Most wedges are designed to be heavier than any other club in the rest of the set—usually two or three swingweight gradations heavier—so they can keep momentum through deeper grass or sand. I've seen some players drill some weight out from behind the sole to make the head lighter, for more feel, while other players like a more substantial-feeling head. That's a matter of personal preference. It doesn't have any effect on how the club actually performs. I modified the bounce on my sand wedge so that I can get the most versatility out of one club. I ground some material away near the heel of the club, so that if I need to hit a shot from a really tight, hard lie, I can just lower my hands and hit the ground with the heel of the club. If I play the shot from a normal position, I still get the full benefit of 12 degrees of bounce.

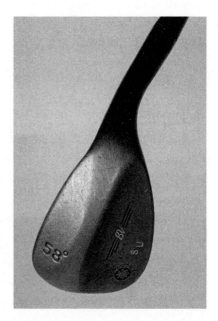

To make my 58-degree wedge more versatile, I had material ground off the bounce on the heel so that I could lower my hands and use that part of the sole for hardpan shots. You've got to work hard to get Bob Vokey to put your initials on your wedge.

The way I determined the specific lofts of my three wedges was totally based on how far I can comfortably hit each one from the fairway. Every tour player has a pet distance he likes to lay up to if he can't get to the green. I like to be between 80 and 85 yards away, and my 58-degree club goes that distance with a smooth swing. If I carried a 60-degree club, I couldn't hit it that far comfortably. And once you start laying up 60 or 70 yards short, it feels like you probably should have gone for the green. For me, 85 yards seems to be the best compromise between laying up and being close enough to feel like I should be getting up and down almost every time. I can hit my gap wedge 105 yards, and my pitching wedge 115 to 120 yards with a smooth swing. For comparison, Ernie Els uses a similar three-wedge configuration—48 degrees, 55 degrees and 59 degrees—but carries his clubs 141 yards, 127 yards and 110 yards. It's nice to be six-foot-four and 220 pounds.

My Vokey wedge has what are called spin-milled grooves. They're cut with a special saw that gives them more grip on the ball, which creates more backspin. On a full shot from the fairway, you want to be able to spin the ball, especially on tour-caliber greens that run hard and fast. The harder-cover balls we play now actually wear out the grooves on a wedge faster than balatas did. If you're practicing and playing a lot, you might change wedges once or twice a year. I don't play as much now but I still go through at least two wedges a year, where I might keep a putter in play for five or six years and irons in the bag for a year or two. Tiger Woods goes through three or four lob wedges in a year not because he wears out the grooves, but because he actually wears the bounce off the bottom of the club. He's a serious short-game practicer. The sandy soil in Florida is also harder on clubs than dirt up in the Midwest or Northeast. It acts like sandpaper, scraping bits of metal off the bottom of your clubs as you use them.

The combination of improvements in wedge and ball technology since I first came out on tour is really dramatic. When I started out, I had what were then considered to be the best wedges you could buy, along with a balata-covered ball that just spun like crazy. Those old Pings had U-shaped grooves, and I could really spin the ball (even sometimes when I didn't want to) when I had a clean lie. You probably remember guys hitting short wedge shots in the early and mid-1990s and having them spin back all the way off the green. That was from the balls and equipment in those days.

The huge difference now is in how the grooves are built. They're box-shaped now, with really sharp edges. They've really done some fine-tuning on the soles of the clubs, too, so they cut through grass much better. All the way through the bag, you can get more spin on the ball from the rough than you could ever get before. On short-game shots, you also get a more consistent flight off the face. I don't like to put a lot of backspin on my chip shots, but I like that the amount of backspin on my wedges is consistent. I don't get one coming out really hot, another checking up because it has a lot of spin, and another one knuckling out of there with no spin at all. What I'm saying is that it doesn't really matter what brand of wedge you buy, but getting a set of recent-model premium wedges is going to give you a big boost over that ten-year-old sand wedge that came with your set.

You're probably thinking that it's fine to talk about hitting wedges from the fairway, or using them to play chip shots, but what about sand shots? Even if you feel reasonably comfortable hitting a pitch or a chip, you probably get a little nervous when you start thinking about the club you use from a greenside bunker. The problem is that most players—and I include some tour players in that group—don't understand *why* a sand wedge works the way it does, or how changing some characteristics of your sand club can influence the way you play a sand shot.

Once you understand the benefits that a good sand wedge can provide from the bunker, it becomes much easier to work on the fundamentals of your actual sand-shot swing (which we'll talk about in detail in Chapter 6). This is where the bounce angle on your wedge becomes particularly important. We've already talked about how a club with little or no bounce (three or six degrees) won't skip through the sand. Lie angle is important here, too, because a club that's too upright won't sit level to the ground. If your club is built too upright, the toe of the club will be up in the air and the heel will dig into the ground. That makes it very hard to hit a good shot.

With my 58-degree club, I can comfortably hit a 20- to 30-yard blast shot, because I know the club isn't going to dig too deep in the sand no matter how hard I swing. If I used less bounce, I'd have to be a lot more careful and a lot more precise. With a club that has less bounce, you run a greater risk of having the club dig in, and then the club can slide right underneath the ball.

When I'm giving a short-game clinic and I start to explain bounce to average players, I can usually see that they have no idea about what bounce really means. But as soon as I can get them to feel the back of the club slide through the sand, they'll immediately talk about how easy it is to get the ball out. The bounce is there to make things more consistent and predictable for you. That's why tour players would much rather miss into a greenside bunker than into the rough. The sand is more predictable than the deep grass because you can spin the ball out of it, and the bounce on the wedge makes a bunker a shot a much more predictable shot.

One part of the equipment puzzle that has changed quite a bit over the last ten years is the ball. New balls are made with multiple covers that make them spin less off the driver—so the ball doesn't curve left or right as much—but spin a lot on short-iron shots, to give you control on firm greens. The knock on multiple-cover balls was always that they felt too hard on finesse shots around the green. That's changed in the last few years, and the top-end balls like the Titleist Pro V1 have a nice, consistent feel, and they perform as well as the soft-cover balls I used in the 1980s. And in reality, feel is the only consideration you need to worry about when it comes to hitting shots around the green. The technique I teach promotes hitting shots with a minimum amount of backspin. You will rely more on the trajectory to control the shot, rather than spin. So it doesn't really matter if you're using a soft, multiple-cover tour ball or a harder game-improvement ball when you hit chips the way I teach. What matters is if you like the way the ball feels as it comes off the club, and it's giving you consistent performance. Predictability is a great thing when it comes to short game.

Does this mean you need to go out and buy all new wedges? Maybe, maybe not. It could mean you just need to have the ones you already have bent a little bit. Start with the pitching wedge in your full set. Get that measured to make sure the lie angle isn't too upright for you. After that, you're going to want two wedges with some separation between them in terms of loft. For me, having a 48-degree pitching wedge, 52-degree gap wedge and 58-degree sand wedge is a perfect combination, with no gaps. Some tour players, like Jim Furyk, go with a four-wedge combination. Jim eliminated his 4-iron, bent his other irons to close that gap in his set, then added an extra wedge between his pitching wedge and lob wedge. His pitching wedge is 46 degrees, his gap wedge 50 degrees, his sand wedge 56 degrees, and his lob wedge 60 degrees. He carries his pitching wedge 130 yards, while he hits the 60-degree club 85. On the women's side, Paula Creamer carries two hybrid clubs, but she still carries four wedges—48-, 50-, 54-, and 60-degree clubs. Her pitching wedge flies 119 and her lob wedge goes 83.

If you don't have enough of a gap between your wedges in terms of loft—or your lie angles are wrong—it's relatively easy to bend them to have more or less. You don't necessarily have to go out and buy new ones.

....

A standard sand wedge is 56 degrees, and that's a decent club to have, as long as you get one with eight to ten degrees of bounce on it. Most likely, you already have one of those in your bag (or in your garage). Given what you're going to learn in the next few chapters, I think you'll find you don't need a 60-degree club to hit lofted shots around the green.

If I were putting together a set of clubs for a 10- or 15-handicapper, here's what I'd include, complete with the lofts for each one.

Driver	(10.5 degrees)
3-wood	(15 degrees)
5-wood	(18.5 degrees)
3-hybrid	(20 degrees)
4-hybrid	(24 degrees)
5-iron	(28 degrees)
6-iron	(32 degrees)
7-iron	(36 degrees)
8-iron	(40 degrees)
9-iron	(44 degrees)
PW	(48 degrees)
GW	(53 degrees)
SW	(56 or 58 degrees)
Putter	(4 degrees)

Statistics clearly show that birdies and par saves are made from shots hit within 120 yards of the flag. Even though I mostly use my 58-degree club within 80 yards, I think it's important to have three and maybe even four wedges in the bag. It's clearly an advantage to be able to make a smooth wedge swing and feel confident that you have three or four yardages covered. To accomplish this, it may mean having wider gaps between your hybrid and long iron clubs. This shouldn't pose much of a problem, since they're not really scoring clubs anyway.

CHAPTER 4
THE ART OF CHIPPING

· ·

O f all the shots you're going to learn in this book, the basic chip shot is certainly the most useful. The average player uses a chip shot—which I define as a shot where you're reducing the loft on your wedge as opposed to trying to use the bounce on the bottom of the club—more than any other short-game shot aside from a putt.

Think about it. The average 12-handicapper might hit three or four greens in regulation per round. That leaves fourteen or fifteen holes where one of three things usually happens: He hits a bad tee shot and has to punch out of trouble and regroup (or take a drop); he hits a decent tee shot and hits a bad approach shot into the bunker or to pitch distance; or he simply misses the green with his approach shot. In any of those circumstances, aside from hitting it into the bunker (which we're also going to cover . . . don't worry), he's in position to hit a chip.

I'd estimate that the average 12-handicapper hits eight or ten chip shots of various lengths in a round. I'd also say that he might get up and down once or twice out of those ten chances. Consistently taking three (or more) shots to get down from 10 yards off the green is the single biggest reason players don't break 90. It's as simple as that. The comparison works at every level of the game, too. The guys at the top of the money list on the PGA Tour have good short games and make a lot of putts. Every guy out there hits it good. The difference comes in how they take advantage of scoring opportunities—and how they save shots when they miss greens.

Improving your chipping skill—to where you're legitimately upset if you don't get up and down—is a very quick way to really reduce your scores. You can make a lot of routine pars by chipping well after just missing a green, and you can salvage great bogeys on those holes where you hit a sketchy pitch shot after punching out from the trees. The math is pretty simple.

Tiger Woods, Vijay Singh, and Phil Mickelson were the top three money earners on the PGA Tour in 2005. They all were also in the top 15 in scrambling a statistic that measures the percentage of times a player makes par or better after missing a green in regulation—on the tour that year. Singh was second, getting up and down 64.2 percent of the time—which is remarkable when you consider the fact that he isn't known as a great putter. He actually finished 60th in putting in '05. Mickelson did it 62.4 percent of the time, and Tiger was at 62.1. Those numbers are phenomenal when you consider how hard tour setups are. Pins are tucked close to the edges of the green and tight to bunkers, and you're in deep, deep trouble if you short-side yourself in heavy rough. The average player on the tour was at about 58 percent, and the stragglers were at about 51 percent. Four percentage points may not seem like a lot, but it's a shot per tournament, and it's the difference between earning $10 million and $1 million.

It's certainly a realistic goal for you to get up and down from around the green 50 percent of the time—regardless of whether you're trying to get up and down for par or bogey. If you can get up and down 50 percent of the time instead of 10 percent of the time, you're going to take three to five shots off your handicap.

A good chipping game expands the effective size of every

This is a chip shot, so my arms don't swing very much. My ball position is up near my left heel, and I have a slight forward press (1). My weight is forward, toward the target. I start the club away with virtually no grip swing (2)—see how the butt end of the club stays in relatively the same spot.

My hips turn a little (3)—my pants legs have more wrinkles than when I started, which shows that turn. When I get to the top of my swing, my hands still don't pass my right leg (4).

On the downswing, my knees turn back around into a squatting position (5), and the lag in my right wrist increases. At impact, the shaft is leaned forward, toward the target, which reduces the loft of the club. Even a foot past impact (6), my right wrist is still holding quite a bit of that lag.

At finish, my left elbow has folded around my body (7), and I've pivoted all the way through. Notice how my knees have still maintained their flex, and my right knee has turned toward my left knee.

Compare this address position to the one for the chip shot before. There's very little shaft lean toward the target (1). My stance is still narrow, with my weight slightly forward. My ball position is just inside my left heel from that narrow stance. The clubhead still starts away first (2)—it has the greatest distance to travel.

My right wrist starts to load and cock (4), which adds more power to the shot, and my right elbow moves back along my side. There's a definite top of the backswing and turn back through the ball (5), and the club comes back through from the inside (5).

5

6

By the time I get to impact, everything is neutral and in line, like it was at address (6). See how my body continues to pivot (7)? My belt is actually turned toward the target at this point.

At the finish (8), my hips have turned all the way, and my left elbow has moved to the side of my body. My hands haven't swung out very wide, and they've stayed close to my body. In this entire sequence, notice how I've kept my weight favoring my left side. My hips turn very level, and the clubhead speed comes from a bigger pivot.

green you look at, because you start looking at a basic chip as something no different than a long putt. To be honest, there are times I'd *rather* have a basic chip shot than a long putt, because I can carry my chip shot over some of the breaks in the green and take a lot of the read out of the equation.

So why do so many players struggle with this bread-and-butter shot? I believe it's mostly because they've got the wrong idea about how to approach it. For some players, the loft on a wedge is intimidating around the green. The idea that you actually have to swing with some speed and trust the loft of the club to get the ball in the air brings all these ideas of blading it or chili-dipping it to mind. So what happens? I see so many players grab a 7-iron or 8-iron, play the ball back in the stance, open way up and swing with a big tilt. They don't use any lower-body pivot, and they yank the grip straight back and straight through.

When you do that, the club goes back straight outside the target line, and the only way to hit it is to tilt your shoulders back, away from the ball, and scoop at it with your hands. If you're going to do that, you might as well just take your putter and use a big swing with that. It's really no wonder players struggle with that chipping setup, because it's effectively robbing you of whatever athletic ability and touch you might have.

As I said in the chapter about basics, what I'm trying to do is to get your short game in line with what you do in a full swing—keep the club moving on plane, make the clubhead end move more than the grip end—and let you take advantage of your athletic sense. In chipping, that starts with the setup.

A chipping stroke is simply the hitting area of a full swing. If you could see a video of your full swing from the waist down, during the time your hands are below your waist, you'd find the chipping move. The only modifications are a narrower stance and your weight distributed to your front foot for the entire shot. When I stand over a full iron shot with my 7-iron, my feet are hip to shoulder-width apart. For a chip, my feet are usually about the width of a clubhead apart—four to five inches. More importantly, I don't open my stance at all, or turn my foot out toward the target.

For some reason, a lot of players when confronted with the smaller swing that a chip shot requires get bunched up close to the ball and squeeze the grip tightly, as if that's going to add precision to the shot. Actually, the opposite is true. I like to give myself enough room to allow my arms and the club to fully release in front of me at impact. I stand taller over the shot and play the ball farther away from me, in the same place I'd play it for a regular shot. I want my arms to swing easily in front of me, just like they would for a full shot. You may need to correct your posture (tilt from the hips, not the waist) and stand farther from the ball.

I actually use the pivoting of my lower body to regulate a large portion of the speed that controls how far the shot goes. You don't want to feel like your lower body is encased in concrete, which I see all the time. When you shoot a jump shot in basketball, it's your legs that are generating most of the power in the shot. A chip shot is exactly the same. The lower body is an active part of this shot, without question. I think of my legs as the thrust and my arms as the steering wheel.

The first few times you try this—pivoting with your lower body and letting the clubhead swing—you're going to feel like you have too much power behind the shot. That's going to be scary, and you might get tentative on a few, but give it some time. Remember, you have been using all arms for energy in your short-game shots before, so until you can coordinate taking arm swing out and adding pivot, your swing will be a little strong.

You might be wondering why I use my 58-degree club instead of something with less loft. I've never been a proponent of using lots of different clubs around the green—say, using a 7-iron for a long, running chip and a sand wedge for something closer that requires a high-lofted shot. I think it's easier to develop confidence and touch with one club and adapt your trajectory with your swing, versus learning the feel of half your set to play shots around the green. I also think the 58-degree club is more versatile than a regular iron. Its sole is designed to perform a variety of functions—dig in to the grass if you play with the leading edge forward, skid across if you play the sole more flat, or bounce if you play it more open. You've got way more choices. And once you get the feel for the chip shot I teach, you're not going to be intimidated by the extra loft.

I want my club to bottom out past the ball on a chip, so I make sure to set up with my weight favoring my left side, and I keep it that way throughout the swing. I've found that if you shift back at all on a chip shot, the tendency is to either hang back during the swing (and hit behind the ball), or sway forward and move the bottom of your swing around inconsistently. But just because my weight is forward doesn't mean I'm not making a pivot with my lower body. I'm essentially pivoting around my left leg. The small hip turn on the way back helps get the club moving on the right plane, and then you pivot through and let the action of pivoting propel the club through the ball. You're not making any conscious effort to throw the club through because your body motion is now helping you support the shaft, or creating lag in your wrist and hands. One thing many average players struggle with is getting too active with the right hand in an effort to lift the ball into the air. Pivoting will help take away that impulse to fire the right hand too aggressively.

The sensation I'm feeling during my swing can be described as fold, turn, and hold. What surprises most amateurs when they watch me hit a chip is how little the grip end of the club actually moves. When I hit a chip, the butt end of the grip pretty much stays in place, while I set the clubhead with my hands and right

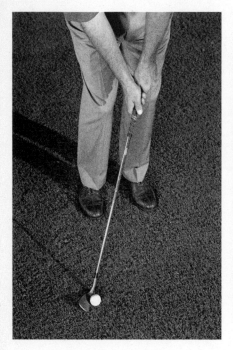 

(ABOVE LEFT) Players have always been taught to set up open to hit a chip shot, with the ball played back in the stance. This encourages a steep backswing outside the target line, and a chopping move down to the ball.

(ABOVE RIGHT) I play my chip shots from a square stance, with the ball just forward of middle. My toe line is square to the target line or even a little bit closed, and my heels are about four inches apart.

elbow. Watching how my elbows work will really give you an idea of how this is different than the way you probably do it. Instead of moving the entire grip back toward my right hip, I slide my right elbow back along my side and make my turn back. The clubhead end moves quite a bit, especially compared to the grip end.

Once I get to the "top" of the backswing—remember, we're talking no more than hip high for most chips—it's just a matter of pivoting through with my lower body first and the shoulders trailing, and letting the club release to the ground at the low point, which I established with my setup. The release of the club simply comes from letting my right elbow lengthen through impact. The sensation of "hold" comes from feeling the angle in my right wrist lag as the club swings through impact. Although my hands are passive on this shot, my forearms rotate smoothly throughout the downswing to assist the de-lofting motion of my wrists. Later on, I'll tell you about some more lofted shots that require you to use a lot more hand action, but for this basic one, quiet hands are what you need.

Before I take you through my own pre-shot process for every chip I hit, let me make one important point about your comfort level. You could well have a shot you like that doesn't fit with the fundamentals I'm talking about here. I don't want you to abandon that shot. I'm certainly not a fan of doing anything that limits your creativity around the green. My goal is just to give you a bunch more options—a chip shot to go with a fringe putt or a bump-and-run 7-iron. By learning a variety of other chip shots, you're armed with some different choices for every situation you face.

And let's talk more about these different situations. How do you know what shot to hit and what factors to take into consideration in your planning? How do you *see* the options in front of you? I'll describe what I do, then give you some advice about how to develop your own process.

As I approach my ball, I certainly take into consideration the lay of the land—if the flag is on the same level as the ball, uphill or downhill, or tucked with not much green to work with—but I'm mostly focused on my lie. Is the ball in the rough, the fringe cut, or the fairway cut? If it's in the rough, is the ball sitting down in the grass, or up on top of the grass? The lie doesn't so much determine what shot I can play as it does what shots I *can't* play.

1

2

5

6

3

4

Notice how I'm leaned left at address. My body will pivot quietly around my left leg all the way through the shot. Look how much the clubhead end moves compared to how little the grip end moves (1, 2, 3). You can also see that there's a definite pivot—look at how my knees move, even on a short shot like this. Heading toward impact, my left wrist is bowed toward the target (5). The club is beginning to de-loft, and my hips are starting to open. The clubhead never gets any higher than my knees.

1

2

5

6

3

4

My feet are slightly closed compared to the rest of my body. Notice how my arms are in front of me—I'm not cramped in too close to the ball. There's room to swing my arms. You can really see the knee action from this angle (4). The pivot happens first, and then my shoulders and the club follow. You can also see the bow in my left wrist after impact (5).

....

What I'm hoping for is a lie in which I don't have to make any special adjustments to try to get clean clubface contact on the back of the ball. If I get it, I'm automatically in offensive mode. I'm trying to make the shot. I'll start by walking up from my ball to the hole to get a sense for how the green breaks. This shot is going to roll like a putt for more than half of its length, so when players simply aim it at the hole I think they're giving away a big source of advantage. An average chip might have three or four feet of break in it. Aiming correctly is the difference between leaving yourself a three-footer or a six-footer. At the tour level, that's the difference between making 85 percent of the putts you have left to making less than half. In other words, it's a big deal.

On my walk to the hole (which I do pretty quickly, so I'm not holding up play), I'm paying particular attention to the area where I want my shot to land. Is the green soft or firm? Is my shot going to kick right? Kick left? Am I chipping into the grain or down grain? If I'm chipping with the grain, I'm going to hit the shot less hard than I am chipping into the grain. My goal is to find a spot to land the ball that's relatively flat and predictable. You don't always get that luxury, but it's what I'm shooting for.

The landing spot I pick is the size of a basketball hoop—pretty precise, but not as precise as a particular blemish on the green or something like that. It's not a dot or a grain or a blemish on the green. From the spot I pick, I'll walk it off and count how many paces it is back to the ball. That's been a part of my routine for more than twenty years—counting the yards to the spot I want the ball to land. I'll literally say "three" to myself if it's 3 yards to the spot I pick and I'm trying to pitch it 9 feet to there. I believe this routine helps my feel on a subconscious level, instead of trying to measure my swing to a shot distance.

Before I play a chip or pitch, I'll actually walk up to the hole from where my ball is to read the terrain and get a sense of where I want to land my shot.

....

Once I have my measurement and my aim, I go into a pre-shot routine, just like I would for a full shot (or even a putt). As I said before, I'm chipping with an attitude. I'm intent on coming as close as possible to jarring the chip. At worse, I'm going to be just a foot or two from the hole. I think it helps to feel that kind of confidence. If you're getting upset when a shot ends up three feet from the hole, that's a sign your short game is getting a lot better. I'm thinking you'll be pretty happy about that.

Taking on that attitude depends on your skill level, for sure. I'd estimate that I'm chipping it with the same attitude you'd have hitting a 10-foot putt. My internal success or failure rate has to do with whether or not it had a chance to go in the hole. If I hit it and the first bounce kicks it two feet left and it never has a chance, that's something that really bothers me. Either I read it wrong or hit it wrong.

One question I get an awful lot is whether to leave the pin in or take it out. I have a strong opinion that the pin does not help good shots. If I want the ball to end up in the hole, I take the pin out. If I can see the hole from where I am, I take the pin out. If I have a downhill shot, or something super hard where I'm going to have trouble managing or predicting the amount my shot is going to roll, I might leave it in. If a shot is really that scary, I might not even chip it, and instead play it with my putter and try to lag it up there.

But if I think my ball is going to come up to the hole rolling like a putt, I want the pin to be out. I've seen lots of good shots dink off of the pin and end up a foot away, and that's certainly enough to drive you nuts. Put it this way: If you had a four-footer you absolutely had to make, with the choice to have the pin in or out, would you leave the pin in? I seriously doubt it. You want the ball to have the best chance to fall into the hole.

If you're in the rough where there will be grass between the face and the ball at impact, and a chip shot is the obvious play, there are a couple of keys to remember. First, the clubhead is more likely to get caught up in the grass, so you have to keep your pivot moving strongly through impact. You also will be contacting the grass first from this lie, so you have to plan for the ball to release more than a cleanly struck chip. Many times from this lie, you will want to consider hitting a pitch shot, which we'll be covering in the next chapter.

Since the contact you make from the rough makes controlling the spin on the ball very tough, this shot is less predictable, and you have to reduce your expectations a little. By far the most common mistake players make from thicker grass is to underestimate how much clubhead speed it takes to get the club through the grass. The result is usually a fluffed chip that moves about three feet. The grass closes down the clubface and you just smother it.

The best way to get a feel for this shot—and judging distance—is to go out to a practice green with a bucket of balls and hit shots. That sounds like obvious advice, but I'm not talking about doing what most people do when they "practice" short game. Standing in the same spot and hitting a bunch of shots aimlessly onto a green without any specific target, or any sense of feedback about whether or not the shot was successful, is only marginally better than not practicing at all. It's really exercise—or work on your tan—more than practice.

You can get tremendous benefit from *one* practice session if all you do is hit three shots after picking a specific landing area and judging how well you did hitting each shot close to the eventual target, then changing to a different target and hitting three more shots, and so on. What you're doing by changing targets is developing the sense of distance control that separates decent chippers from great ones. By moving around the edges of the practice green, you're entering a lot of different lies and situations in your memory banks. When you face that shot out on the course, you won't be too surprised. Bare lie from mostly dirt to a pin on a tier? It's a lot less nerve-racking if you've experimented with that shot at the practice green.

Another thing I like to do before a round is take two balls and drop them into different lies around the practice green, then challenge myself to get up and down. Making a game out of it adds some pressure that isn't there when you're just out by yourself hitting practice shots. It's also fun to pair up with a buddy and have a little up-and-down challenge. It's amazing how your focus improves when bragging rights are involved.

CHAPTER 5

THE ART OF PITCHING

· ·

Your chipping skills are going to help you when the flag is closer to the center of the green, you've got plenty of room to work with, and you've got room to roll the ball up like a putt. As the pin moves more toward the sides of the green, or moves closer to some kind of obstacle like a bunker or a water hazard, your pitching game comes into play. The ability to play a shot with more loft gives you so much more flexibility in how you approach a short-game situation.

First things first: I'd like you to stop thinking of a pitch as simply as a shot for a situation when you're faced with a longer distance to negotiate. It can be that, but that's not all it is. I define a pitch shot as a shot where you're using the bounce on the bottom of the club (instead of the leading edge) and then releasing your hands through impact to make the ball fly up in the air. You can hit a pitch shot from right next to the green to a pin that's only five or six yards on the putting surface, just like you could play a 30-yard chip shot from in front of the green to keep the ball under a really strong wind. It's a difference in how you hit the shot, not in how long it is.

You'll probably hit more chip shots during a given round than pitch shots, but understanding how to loft the ball more in the air is certainly valuable. You're going to have them a lot on holes where you run into problems off the tee and have to lay up with your approach shot. If you can hit some of those pitches close, you're obviously going to take a lot of pressure off your putting game. You're not always going to have a direct path along the ground to hit a chip shot—you might have to carry a bunker, or go over a finger of rough that cuts between one corner of the green and the other. A pitch shot really comes in handy on greens that have a lot of undulation. I'll hit one and completely take out a slope or tier, so I don't have to do as much figuring about what a shot hit lower along the ground would do in terms of break. And just like the chip shot, I'm not trying to put backspin on the ball and control the shot with spin. I'm letting the loft do the work, so that the ball flies high and lands soft. It's a great weapon.

As we talked about in the basics chapter, your setup isn't going to be much different for a pitch shot than it is for a chip. As the shot gets longer, your stance gets a little bit wider. On a short pitch—say 15 yards—my feet will be the same distance apart as they would be on a chip shot, about four inches. Once I get up to a full pitch shot of 40 or 50 yards, my feet are going to be just a bit less than hip-width apart, and not much different than they'd be for a full shot with a wedge.

These are some pretty small swings, and a consistent pivot point is going to help you bring the club back through the impact area consistently every time and give you a lot of precision. Pivoting consistently can be a challenge when you've got two legs to balance on and you're holding the club with two hands. That's why I like to start with my weight to the left, toward the target, and maintain that through my swing. I'm essentially establishing my left leg as a fixed pivoting point down to the ground, and turning around my left leg back and through. You don't need a big weight shift to develop power. We're talking about, at most, a 40-yard shot.

For a pitch shot, my hands are just slightly ahead of the ball at address, and my feet are eight to ten inches apart. As the pitch shot gets shorter, my feet move closer together from shoulder width down to four inches. That makes it easier to keep the swing moving around the pivot.

....

The main thing that will be different in your pitch setup compared to the chip setup is how you set the shaft at address. On a chip shot, your hands are further ahead of the ball, and you're hitting the shot with the grip end of the club leaning forward, with as much as 20 degrees of de-loft toward the target. The club hits the ball first, and then the leading edge of the club comes in contact with the ground. On a pitch shot, the hands are still a bit ahead at address, but the shaft is closer to vertical. You're hitting the ground with the bounce on the bottom of the club and using the loft to send the ball up into the air.

1

2

5

6

My pitching setup is neutral—there's no opening of my toe line or moving the ball back (1). My arms are hanging straight down, too. In frame 3, notice how the club is directly between my arms and parallel to the target line. Before impact, my hips open, but my shoulders stay closed (5). The swing follows the shoulder line, so it's going to the inside. In picture 8, it's obvious that I haven't hung back at all. My chest is up over my left leg.

....

3

4

7

8

In the last chapter, we talked about fold, turn, and hold—the "feels" for a chip shot. On a pitch shot, you're going to feel the first two the same way, sliding the right elbow back along your side as you pivot back, but your hand and wrist action will become a much larger piece of the equation.

Even though my arms are going to get up just above my waist, the butt end of the club is not going to travel very far from where it started when I was at address. I'm adding wrist cock—the hinging of my wrists—which increases the distance the clubhead end of the club travels.

The top of the backswing on a chip is well below the waist. For a 20-yard pitch, however, my arms are going to get waist high and the club will point pretty close to straight up in the air. Just like with the chip, it's then a matter of pivoting through with my lower body first and the shoulders trailing, and letting the club hit the ground at the low point, which I established with my setup. But instead of holding and turning, I'm going to release the club. You're probably asking, what does that mean, exactly?

Let's talk a little bit about the concept of "release," as it relates to pitch shots. On a chip shot, you're pretty much hitting the shot with your pivot, while your elbows simply slide along your sides. Your wrists don't actively unhinge in a big way through impact. On a pitch shot, your wrists work freely in a vertical hinging motion. My analogy is using a sledgehammer with both hands, or driving a nail one-handed. If you apply this wrist action along the right swing plane (I prefer a shallow plane), the clubhead will return back to impact squarely with plenty of speed.

You will need to rotate your forearms during the takeaway in order to set your wrists and hands on-plane. The left wrist will be cupped at the end of your backswing, just as it would be if you raised a sledgehammer straight up in front of you. You want to feel the release of your wrists and clubhead early in the downswing. It may take you a few swings to coordinate your new release with your smooth lower-body pivot in the through swing.

As the club comes through impact, from the face-on view, you'd see the shaft vertical or even tilted a little bit back, away from the target, on a very high shot. The bounce on your sand wedge will skip through the turf cleanly. After impact, your left wrist and elbow will both give way to fully release the clubhead. Your left wrist will cup, and your right palm will stay facing the sky, which means there's almost no forearm rotation in the through swing. Your hands and arms will travel along your body as the left elbow folds just past impact. On most simple pitches, I prefer the hands to finish low as the club finishes left and up, higher than on a chip shot. At this point, I hope you are understanding the relationship between the left-wrist position at impact and the loft on the clubface.

The biggest struggle I see for the average player comes from the impulse to move the arms faster and pull on the grip end of the club on the downswing in an effort to generate clubhead speed. A pitch shot isn't any different than a full swing in that pulling hard on the grip end doesn't necessarily speed up the clubhead. In fact, if you do move the grip end too fast, you'll probably come to impact with an open clubface, which will cause you to hit shots high and short.

How does the grip end get to be moving too fast? Too much arm swing. If you don't turn the right way and use your pivot to develop speed at the clubhead end of the club, you compensate by making a bigger arm swing to try to find the energy to actually hit the ball. When you start making a big arm swing with no body turn, you pull the handle of the club more (and out of

1

2

5

6

Aside from the narrower stance, this setup looks just like my setup for a full shot with a short iron (1). Notice how I'm extending my arms, not getting too close to the ball so that my arms brush against my chest. As the club moves back, notice how it stays on the plane line on which it started. The clubface in picture 3 isn't shut—it's on the same angle as my spine. The leading edge is not supposed to be pointing at the sky. In picture 7, you can see that just past impact, my hands have moved farther left than the clubhead, meaning I've kept the angle in my wrist.

....

3

4

7

8

position), and—most importantly—you lose feel in your hands. When the body works well and you minimize your arm swing, it's incredible how responsive and sensitive your hands get.

Here, the entire shaft is moving away from the ball at the same speed (1). I've got no wrist hinge (2), and the arms shove the grip away from the body, not around it.

Another issue average players often struggle with is shoulder tilt at address. The impulse is to set up with the right shoulder lower than the left shoulder, because it feels like you're going to be able to lift the ball up in the air more easily. What happens is that the right arm gets "short" and bent because of that tilt, and the left arm gets long, hyperextended, and locked. Aside from the obvious problem of scooping at it, this address position also causes you to hinge the club awkwardly on the backswing (if you hinge it at all), and you'll tend to hit the ground behind the ball. Once you hit it fat a couple of times, you'll lift up through impact to try to avoid it, and that's when you'll skull it across the green.

As I said earlier, if I can just get you in a neutral position with your setup and get you to start swinging the clubhead end of the club with some speed, you're going to solve a lot of problems before they even start. The key moment for the average guy (Eureka!) happens when he feels the clubhead unload on the downswing because the wrists actively unhinge. As long as your setup fundamentals are good—weight forward, shoulders level due to a left spine tilt—unloading the clubhead puts the bounce into the turf nicely, and shoots the ball up in the air. After impact, my elbows fold and the clubhead finishes higher, and my hands are in the middle of my chest. If you jerk the grip end through, your hands will finish past your chest.

So how do I control the distance on my pitch shots? The way most players do it is by swinging their arms faster. I do it mostly with the size and speed of my lower-body pivot. My pivot is small and smooth on short shots, and larger with a more aggressive turn through on longer shots. The end effect is that my arms stay at home, close to my body, and the speed required for the shot comes from my pivot speed and the release of the clubhead.

As I said in the chipping chapter, I don't want the grip end of the club moving very far. If you get the idea that you need to make a faster swing with your arms doing most of the work, the first thing that's going to happen is that the pulling action of the left arm will send your left shoulder up, tilt your spine back, away from the target, move the bottom of your swing way behind the ball, and there it is—a fat shot, or a skull from hitting it on the upswing. Think of it as a bigger pivot and you'll start to feel the chain reaction I've been talking about. My arms almost never get up past my waist on a pitch shot as long as 40 yards. You really don't need as much arm swing as you think you do, as long as you're using your lower body effectively.

(ABOVE LEFT) I see this position a lot when a player has been working on keeping his right elbow in front of him. His hands work away from his body, and he often gets the club too inside going back.

(ABOVE RIGHT) This position is a result of keeping the left elbow straight for too long on the through swing. It will tilt the spine back, forcing you to flip your hands at the ball.

When the hands stay more passive and work properly, the right elbow folds back along the right side and the club swings around, not straight back.

On the through swing, the left elbow folds around the side the same way the right one did on the backswing. Notice how my arms have released past my chest.

Your strategy for aiming where the ball is going to land has tremendous impact on how you use your arms and body. When I see players for the first time, I ask them where they're aiming to land their pitch shots. The answer is usually that they haven't come up with a place to land it. They're just looking at the hole. Actually, aiming at the hole is a big problem, because you make this big, giant arm swing with the idea of trying to hit it to the hole, and your brain subconsciously knows you really need to land it short of the hole and account for it rolling up there. The result is a big decelerating move on the downswing and bad contact. A lot of players make the backswing that's appropriate for flying it to the hole, and then have to put on the brakes on the way down so they don't hit it over the green. That's not a good recipe for solid contact.

When I'm planning my pitch shot, I pick a very specific spot to land the ball. I want to fly the ball to a relatively neutral landing spot—preferably one that's pretty flat—and that accounts for how much my shot is going to roll out after it lands. I pick a spot the size of a basketball hoop, and that becomes my focus in terms of target. I'm not even looking at the flag once I pick that spot. Another advantage of focusing on that spot is that it's closer to you than the flag is. It's easier to see, and you can be more precise with your aim when you're going for a target that's closer to you. Once you start picking the right landing spot, you can swing aggressively with the goal of hitting it to that spot, and your problems with decelerating will fade away.

I get a lot a questions about what club to hit on a pitch shot, and if it's better to use a less-lofted club for a longer pitch. I use my 58-degree wedge on virtually every pitch shot I hit, from just off the green to 50 yards out. If you need to switch to a 52-degree wedge to hit a longer pitch, simply plan for the ball not to land as soft as it would with your lofted wedge. If it makes you comfortable to take less of a swing with a club that has less loft, then go for it. If you keep your technique consistent with what I've been talking about in the basics chapter and here, you can hit a pitch shot with any club that has some bounce on the bottom.

I've made the point that I'm in favor of hitting shots that don't rely on backspin to stop next to the hole. Why? Isn't it cool to be able to back it up or make it skid to a stop like tour players do? I'm sure you've seen guys like Tiger Woods or Ernie Els zip a 40-yard pitch shot in there tight with a bunch of backspin, so that the ball just checks up and stops. For sure, that shot looks really flashy, but I'm not sure how necessary it really is. The truth of the matter is, the ability to spin the ball like that has a lot to do with skill level and hand speed and what kind of ball you play. I can't spin the ball and knock it down and make it check up like Woods or Els. They're doing it with the same physics as a full swing—hand speed and lots of lag, which pinches down on the ball. I don't have the hand speed at impact that they do. And honestly, most people don't. That's why I think it's far better to learn how to hit what I call a high, faster-release pitch shot. Those shots hit soft—with more loft on them than drive.

With any new technique, it will take a little time for it to feel comfortable—especially under pressure. If you're used to scuffing shots along the ground with a 7-iron instead of pitching them up in the air, this is going to feel like walking a tightrope for you in the beginning. When you start using more speed in your swing—either in chipping or pitching—I'm sure you're going to start thinking about the possibility of blading it. That's certainly natural. But you need to trust me when I tell you that if you follow the basic fundamentals I'm taking about—weight forward and pivot through impact—you're going to be far *less* likely to blade it than before, even with the increased speed.

One of the reasons that "fundamentals" like the ones those teachers gave me when I was a kid have stood the test of time is because they are the practical application of the most efficient physics of a golf swing. They also give you the most room for error. If you practice keeping your weight forward and making a pivot on your downswing, you're going to increase the width of the bottom of your swing. That means you've got three or four inches at the bottom where you can actually hit the ball and get a decent result. If you're using the bounce correctly, you can hit it a bit fat and the club will slide along the ground and give you a decent result. If you hit it a bit thin, you'll put more backspin on the shot and it'll check up. For me, that's a great kind of security blanket—I know I can make a pretty big mistake and not leave the ball at my feet or whack it over the green. As long as I'm using the bounce on the grass the right way, I can actually hit three inches behind the ball and put the ball on the green 10 or 15 feet from the hole. When shots like that become your "bad" miss—instead of a chili-dip or a screaming blade across the green, you'll really know that the level of your short game has improved.

And as you get more and more comfortable hitting these kinds of pitches—and getting a clear feel of where the bottom of your swing is, which will come pretty fast—your confidence will grow. And as you get the feel for where the bottom of your swing is, you'll be able to expand your short-game control over a whole variety of short-game and trouble shots. Because once you understand how bounce works and how to consistently use it to your advantage, you'll truly become a dangerous player.

CHAPTER 6

THE ART OF
SAND PLAY

. . . .

I've always been fascinated by the sort of "split personality" that bunker shots have in golf. Tour players are obviously more comfortable than the average guy on any shot in the game, but with bunker play, it's like they're playing a completely different sport.

Sure, a nasty downhill, buried lie in the sand will stress any player out, but a good player actually looks forward to hitting a bunker shot from a good lie. The reaction I get when I watch players in my clinics is the complete opposite. You can see the apprehension on a player's face before he even gets into the bunker to show me how he hits it. The swings are usually tentative stabs, followed by a couple of balls bladed over the green, a couple fluffed two or three feet, or both.

Many, many average players are completely intimidated—or even terrified—by the sand. They might have heard a few boilerplate bunker tips somewhere, like open the stance and clubface way up or hit two inches behind it, and they just swing down at it and hope the ball somehow comes out of there.

Why is it that a tour player who sees his shot heading toward missing the green actually *hopes* his ball goes in the bunker, while the average player is actively rooting for his to go any-where but the sand? It comes from the average player's basic mis-understanding of how to get the ball to come out of the sand. Once you get how the sand wedge's design can help you hit a bunker shot, all it takes is a feel for how to release the clubhead into the sand and you will get the ball out every single time. It's as close to a magic bullet as I've seen in golf.

Tour players know this, and they know that they'll almost always get a more consistent lie in sand—which has been mani-cured and raked—than in rough around the green. They also know that they can hit a shot with spin on it out of sand—some-thing that's hard to do from deep grass. As a result, the best tour players get up and down more than 60 percent of the time from *all* bunkers around the green. From a good lie on a straightforward bunker shot, that number goes up to more than 80 percent. In fact, tour players are so good out of the sand that some tournament organizers have started experimenting with rakes that have thick teeth, to make bunker surfaces more irregular and more difficult to hit from. Jack Nicklaus did it for his Memorial Tournament in 2006, and players hated it. That's probably a good indication that you'll see more of it in tourna-ment golf in the future. Luckily for you, though, recreational golfers will probably only have to deal with the occasional foot-print or bad rake job.

Once you get the feel for how the club's bounce angle wants to work through the sand—if you just let it—you'll simply be amazed at how easy it is to hit a sand shot. Your attitude about the sand will completely change, and that will have positive ef-fects on the rest of your game. Instead of looking at an approach shot and worrying about what happens if you miss right, into the bunker, you'll be able to go for your shots with the knowl-edge that if you hit it in the sand, you can probably get out with-out too much fuss. You'll be amazed at how much touch you'll discover once you're not worried simply about getting out of the sand.

Everything I teach about the bunker shot, from the setup to the swing, is designed to get the bounce on the back of the wedge working the way it was designed to. You'll remember from the equipment chapter what we talked about when it comes to bounce. The extra metal on the back of the club works to keep the club from digging down into the sand. It works as a skid to help the club skip along the top of the sand instead, like a rock or a boat skimming across the water. What you're trying to do is put that skid in position to do that through the three or four inches of contact area in the sand. Let's talk a little bit about how to do that.

The first thing to do is to forget about what you might have heard about how to hit a sand shot. You know, the part about playing the ball forward and opening your stance, aiming way to the left of the target, picking the club up to the outside, and swinging on an outside-to-in path. I'm not trying to tell you that that technique doesn't work. A lot of players on tour use it, and you can have success with it. It's a "safe" technique. But it is not what the best players are doing. My view has always been that the simplest way to do something—the way that requires the fewest manipulations and the most room to make a mistake without it hurting you—is the way to go. The genius of Seve Ballesteros or Gary Player is that the technique they used was so simple and efficient.

I started out hitting bunker shots the way I just described, but the summer before I finished college at Missouri, Tom Pernice showed me a whole different way to hit bunker shots, and it was so much easier and consistent. Better yet, it let me use the touch and instincts I have. The setup and swing I'm going to talk about here probably won't sound like anything you've ever heard before. That's okay. You'll be the only one in your foursome using it, and you'll be the only guy consistently getting up and down from the sand. When they ask, just make sure you make them go out and buy their own copies of this book!

First, get it out of your head that the ball has to be way forward and your stance should be way open. As hard as it might be to believe, if you have a generic 30-foot bunker shot, you should be setting up square to your target line. Your feet should be spread very wide apart—even wider than driver width. Your knees are going to bow out slightly, almost as if you're sitting in a chair. Ball position is under your left armpit. It's forward of middle, but definitely not in front of your left heel, like it would be for a "conventional" sand shot. The clubface should be square to slightly open, but not laid out flat and completely open like you've probably heard (unless you're under the lip or something). Setting it up more square gives you more effective bounce angle to use. You're going to set up relatively far from the ball, and your hands are going to be lower—closer to the ground—than you've probably ever had them before for a golf swing.

Setting your spine angle is a crucial part of the setup process. If you're set up open, with the ball way forward, the tendency is to drop your right shoulder. This encourages you to dig the club into the sand too far behind the ball, or worse yet, blade it over the green when you try to compensate for that. In the method I teach, your spine is tilted slightly *left*, toward the target. Your weight is definitely on the left foot, and it should stay there throughout the swing. One note of caution is in order here: When I tell somebody to tilt his weight forward, his first move is almost always to slide his hips toward the target and tilt his spine *back*, away from the target. Try this to get the feel of this spine tilt right: Set up with your feet shoulder-width apart and bend your knees. Hold your club in your right hand. Now slide your left hand down the side of your left leg until you touch your left knee. You'll have a nice spine tilt to the left.

(ABOVE LEFT) Notice how wide my stance is compared to the chip and pitch shots. Ball position is slightly forward from center, and my hands are behind the ball. My shoulders and hips are level.

(ABOVE RIGHT) I see this setup position far too much—spine tilted to the right, ball too far forward, and feet aimed to the left of the target.

(BOTTOM RIGHT) To get the feel for setting your weight to the left and keeping the shoulders level instead of leaning back, hold the club in front of you in your right hand and slide your left hand down your leg. Once it gets to your knee, then move it over and take your left-hand grip. You might even exaggerate the left shoulder position and hit some shots with it low to get the feel for it.

With my spine tilted slightly left (and my weight on my left side), I actually set up with my hands back, behind the ball. In other words, the angle of the shaft is pointed back, away from the target, about an inch. It's not dramatic, but it's definitely back and not at 90 degrees. This increases the effective loft of the club dramatically, and fully exposes the bounce. You're able to set up square to the target and aim exactly where you want to hit it, without opening your stance and the clubface and having to calculate for a lot of sidespin.

When I actually swing the club, I'm making a very narrow swing, not a wide one like you would on a full shot. I'm essen-

This is a typical bunker mistake leaning back through impact to try to help the ball in the air. It causes inconsistent contact—one shot fat, then another one thin.

tially just lifting my hands up and down while adding a turn to it. The goal is to add speed on the clubhead end without adding speed on the grip end. It's like snapping a towel. If you move both ends of the towel, you can't snap one end. You want to keep the hands and wrists close to the body throughout your swing— not extend them away from you on the backswing like a full shot. On the backswing, the left wrist cups (bends in toward the body), as opposed to bowing back, away from the body.

Your right elbow slides back along your right side as you turn your hips. You're going to keep your weight left, so that's definitely going to feel like a reverse pivot. After that, you simply

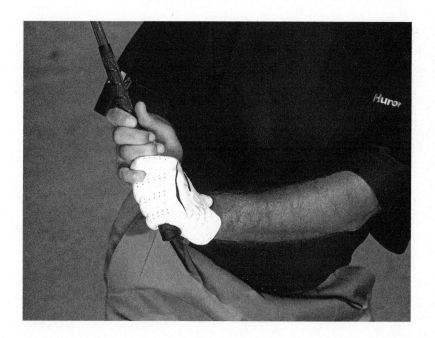

On a bunker shot, the left wrist has a lot of "cup," meaning it curves upward from the joint where the hand connects to the arm. The cupped wrist adds bounce and loft to the shot.

throw the clubhead and slap the sand. You want your clubhead to pass your hands before you hit the ball. The grip stops before impact, so you're putting "up" on the ball rather than "drive," which comes from moving the grip with more speed, like you do on a full shot. Like any other shot, you want to resist trying to scoop the ball in the air with your hands. Hitting down on it with speed is what makes the shot go up in the air.

You want to stop the grip end and release the arms and club and keep your right shoulder up while you do. If you let your shoulder dip, you're not going to be able to throw the clubhead through with any speed. If you stay left and keep your shoulder from dipping, you're going to hit nice, high shots. Then, if you want to hit it a little longer, say 25 or 30 yards, you simply add a little bit more arm swing, or even change to your 52-degree wedge.

By keeping my spine tilt the same throughout the swing, I can hit the sand much more precisely—right where my head is positioned. When you lean back at address or make a big weight shift back and then through, the spot you hit in the sand can vary by as much as five or six inches. That's just not consistent. One time, you'll hit it really fat and short, and the next time you'll hit really close to the ball and hit it too far. Once you get stable on your left side, you can really control where you hit the sand and do some different things with your shots by making slight changes in your ball position. The closer I hit to the ball and the more acceleration I swing the clubhead with, the higher the shot will go and the more it will spin.

(OPPOSITE) I take a wide stance with my feet turned out (1), because it helps me pivot back and through. You can see how much the clubface opens early in the backswing (3), and how it stays open through the top of the backswing. I'm definitely turning (4), but my body position doesn't change. I'm not sliding back at all. My weight stays on my left leg through the downswing and the club gets really shallow (5). After impact, the club doesn't rotate at all. My right palm is still facing up toward the sky (6).

1

2

3

4

5

6

7

8

1

2

5

6

The striking thing about these pictures is how much sand gets moved on a standard bunker shot. I once heard that you could fill an eight-ounce glass with the sand you need to move on this shot, and I believe that. You can really see here how my elbows fold (7) close to my sides. The speed comes from wrist action and arm speed, not from a big body move.

3

4

7

8

1

2

3

4

5

6

7

I start out with my hands very low, which flattens the shaft angle and increases the effective loft of the club (1). On the way back, the club moves up and outside the plane line slightly (2). Notice how level my shoulders stay through impact. I don't drop my right shoulder at all to try to help the ball into the air.

It's important to talk about path at this point. When you hit a conventional bunker shot, you're cutting across the ball, and it will tend to spin and kick to the right when it lands. When I hit my bunker shot—with a square path where the club comes inside the target line on the way back, moves square to the target line through impact, and then comes back inside the target line after impact—my ball will spin back straight, right toward me. I believe this is a more precise way to play bunker shots, and your average result is going to be better. The only thing hard about learning to hit shots with my method is overcoming the idea that you need to pull on the grip end when you swing. Most of the time, it only takes a short "get to know you" period before you're hitting it great.

Let me take you through how I approach a bunker shot, step by step. This will give you an idea of how I think about the shot, and how different lies in the sand impact how you play it. The lie is always the first thing I check. You can feel the difference in the conditions when you step into the bunker, just by how the sand reacts to your feet. If you're basically walking on top of the sand, with your feet not making much of an impact, you're dealing with super-firm sand. Your feet will sink right into fluffy sand. When you dig your feet in for stability in your stance, you can feel the consistency of it once you get below the top layer. Oftentimes the top layer of sand will be wet from rain or dew, but just below, it's fluffy. That secondary layer is what you need to worry about.

After feeling the sand with my feet, I look at the ball. Is the ball sitting on top of the sand, where I can get some grooves on it and make it spin? Is it sitting down, where I need to take more sand and account for the fact that it will run out? What is the sand like? I use my feet to do that. Is it hard? Fluffy? Grainy? If the sand is fluffy, I'm going to hit farther from the ball and swing faster. The club is going to dig more in fluffy sand. If I dig my feet in and the sand is firm and thin, I need to swing not as fast and hit closer to the ball. If you tilt to the right on hard sand, you're almost guaranteed to hit the sand too early and bounce the club into the back of the ball.

In each kind of sand, you can end up with a different kind of lie. In soft, powdery sand, a shot hit into the bunker with a lot of loft will tend to leave you with your ball sitting in a little sand crater created when it hit. You have to swing more aggressively and hit farther behind the ball in that situation. In wetter sand, that high shot coming in could actually plug or bury, which is really a problem. Then you've got to gouge the ball out the best you can and play for a lot of roll. The best lies come from when the ball bounces or rolls into the bunker and stays on top of the sand.

From a tour player's perspective, my least favorite kind of lie is a kind of in-between one, where the ball isn't buried but isn't sitting up, either. I say that because if I have a standard lie in a standard bunker, I fully expect to hit a great shot—within two or three feet of the hole. If I have a really terrible lie, where the ball is buried, or I'm up against the back lip of the bunker, I'm not going to feel too bad about a mediocre result because my expectations aren't as high.

Once I've diagnosed the lie, I'm thinking about what the ball is going to do when it hits the green. How close I hit to the ball is going to determine how much the ball checks up when it lands. If you hit very close to the ball (you almost never want to actually hit the ball itself), there's only a thin layer of sand between the clubhead and the ball. That creates a lot of friction on the ball, and it will check up when it lands, or even back up a little bit. If you hit further away from it, the ball basically comes out on a pillow of sand, without as much friction.

How close is close to the ball? On a basic, straightforward shot, I'm hitting about an inch behind the ball. If I need the ball to spin more, I'm hitting closer to it. If it's a pressure situation and I'm worried about how precisely I can strike the sand, I can hit farther away from it for more margin of error, then just account for the additional roll the ball will have. But with my method, there's never going to be a huge amount of roll, because the things you're doing with your setup are designed to make the ball come out pretty high. A high shot is going to land pretty softly no matter what you do.

I'm going to tell you more about trouble shots in the bunker—like buried lies, and shots from the back lip where you have to stand half in and half out of the bunker—in the next chapter. But let's go over what to do when you're confronted with some less-than-perfect lie situations.

A slight uphill lie is actually easier to deal with than one that's perfectly flat, because the incline is automatically going to give you more loft on the shot. As the lie gets more dramatically uphill, you have to account for it by swinging a little bit harder. The higher your shot goes, the shorter it goes, so a dramatic uphill lie will tend to produce a higher, shorter shot. The key is to not get too active with your body, because you'll lose your balance. On a steep uphill shot, I'm trying to pinch pretty close to the ball in the sand and hit down on it—to the point that the club sticks in the slope after impact.

A downhill lie is more problematic, because you'll have the tendency to hang back on your right side to keep your balance through the swing. Hanging back is never good on a bunker shot, and it's especially bad on one from a downhill lie, because you'll either bury the club in the slope or blade it over the green. You really need to concentrate on staying left with your spine tilt and swinging more down to follow the slope. The shot is going to come out lower and it's not going to spin as much as it would from a flat lie. If you're a confident bunker player, you can swing faster to try to produce a little more spin to stop the shot, but that's risky.

The rules for sidehill lies are similar to those you'd follow on a full shot. If the ball is above your feet, play it a little more in the middle of your stance and expect to pull it a little bit left of the target. When I have that shot, I flatten my swing more like a baseball swing and open the face a little to account for it, and I end up hitting it pretty straight. When the ball is below your feet, you need to flex your knees more than normal and tilt over more from your hips to get to the ball at address, and then retain that tilt through the swing. You also want to swing a little steeper, or upright, because of the shaft angle at address. You'll tend to push this shot a little. I don't recommend shutting the face to compensate for it. I'll just aim a little bit left.

What I like about the bunker technique I teach is that it really increases the average result of the shots you hit. Even if you aren't as precise as you can be with how you hit your shot, just by getting the bounce moving the right way, you almost can't hit a really horrible shot. Hit too far behind it and you'll pop the ball out and leave it short. Hit a little close to the ball and you'll hit it longer, but it will spin more and check up. And unless you've got a seriously funky lie, you can pretty much forget about the nasty bladed shots you used to hit over the green. And that's not such a bad thing.

In Chapter 9, I've put together a variety of bunker drills that will get you feeling how the clubhead loads and unloads on a good bunker shot, and how to get your shots splashing out much more easily and consistently. It won't take much more than an hour of practice time with these drills before you'll be hitting your bunker shots much more consistently—and consistently closer to the hole.

CHAPTER 7
TROUBLE SHOTS

. . . .

T he same thing that makes a short-game practice area so great—acres of nice, flat turf with an unlimited supply of balls (that don't count against your score)—is also its biggest limitation. Because, as I'm sure you've discovered the hard way, you don't always get perfect lies when you're out playing on the course.

Ironically, this is actually more true for the average guy than it is for a tour player, at least in terms of things like divots and hardpan. When I play in a PGA Tour event, I'm going to see every golf course in the best condition it's going to be in all year. The grass is almost always perfect, and the only "trouble" shots I'm going to have to deal with are usually ones that I get myself into—rough and nasty lies in the corners of bunkers. Look at what Phil Mickelson did at the PGA Championship in 2005. In the final round, he hit his second shot on the par-5 18th hole into deep grass next to the green. He had a tough lie, but he was able to hit a nice 50-foot explosion shot from the grass to two feet and win the tournament.

But in real golf, the kind you play every week at your home course, you're going to have to deal with a variety of less-than-perfect situations. Rough is the most basic, if you miss the green in deep grass. A flat lie from the rough is challenging enough, and you'll certainly have to deal with uphill, downhill, or side-hill lies from that grass. You've also got bare lies, where the grass hasn't grown completely in, or hardpan in the summer. Divots are an especially frustrating problem, because it usually feels like you didn't do anything wrong to deserve the bad break. I've been in tournament situations where I walked up to my ball 20 yards short of the green in fairway grass and saw it sitting down in a giant divot hole. That will challenge your ability to keep cool.

Bunkers present their own kinds of diabolical opportunities to get into trouble. Like I said in the chapter on bunker play, the basic, flat, good lie in the bunker is one of the most favorable places you can be aside from on the green, because of your ability to control the spin on the ball out of sand. But if the ball settles in its own pitch mark in the bunker, or worse yet, buries, you've got some extra work to do. You also need to know how to deal with a situation when your ball comes to rest up near the edge of the bunker and you have to either get the ball up in the air fast or stand with one foot in and one foot out of the bunker.

Let's take some of these situations one by one, and I'll walk you through.

DEEP ROUGH

When I say deep rough, I'm talking about grass where you're not going to be able to make clean contact between the club and the ball. The standard cut of rough you'd see just off the green at the average public course doesn't qualify, unless the ball is really nestled down in the grass. (Remember, if you can make decent contact with the ball, you can hit the same basic chip or pitch shots I've been telling you about over the last few chapters.)

From the deeper grass, I play a blast shot that's virtually identical to a sand shot we talked about in the last chapter. The concept is the same—sending the bounce of the club skidding through the grass (instead of sand) so that the ball pops out in a cloud of grass shavings. The only difference is a subtle one—when I take it back in the bunker, my backswing is slightly steeper. I swing a little shallower from the grass because the ground doesn't give as much as the sand does. Just like with the bunker shot, my stance gets way, way wider than for a chip. My feet are at least a foot and a half apart—maybe even two and a half feet apart if I have to get really low to blast one out of a nasty lie. My hand position is really low, down at knee level, and I move a lot farther from the ball. You need to start with your left wrist cupped, and bring it back with a lot of wrist cock, right away. The downswing is simple. You're throwing the clubhead as hard as you can, with the goal of getting it to pass the grip end through impact. In the bunker, the goal is to hit an inch or two behind the ball, but on the deep-grass shot, I'm trying to hit three or four inches behind and power the clubhead through the grass. Grass provides more resistance than sand, so you need some speed on the clubhead, and there's definitely a lot of speed on the clubhead relative to how far you're trying to hit the ball. You're trying to swing with loft so that the club cuts through the grass but still hits a high, soft shot that doesn't require much spin to stop. When you get 15 or 20 yards away with this shot, you're going to need almost three quarters of full clubhead speed. I might hit a 10- or 15-yard shot with the volume of swing that I'd make from a good lie 50 or 60 yards away.

(ABOVE LEFT) When the ball nestles down in the rough, you can't catch the back of it cleanly with your wedge. As a result, the ball won't spin very much, and you'll have to stop it with loft.

(ABOVE RIGHT) If the ball sits on top of the rough, you can get spin on the shot, but you have to be careful not to swing under the ball.

Mickelson is just tremendous at these shots, because he's got both the technique and the courage to hit it under pressure. I've seem him hit a 20-foot pitch from deep grass with a swing that would hit the ball 75 yards from a good lie in the fairway. Miss that a little too close to the ball and he's looking at hitting it over the gallery and into the next fairway.

Consider yourself lucky if your ball comes to rest on top of the deep grass instead of nestled down in it. You'll be able to get a club on the ball and use a more conventional chip or pitch shot, but you still have to be careful. There's a cushion of grass under the ball, and if you swing too deeply into the grass, you can easily swipe the club completely under the ball. It compounds your problem, because the ball will usually drop back down into the divot you just made. If you're going to make a mistake, it's better to catch this shot a little bit thin. It will spin a bit more, which controls some of the distance.

1

2

3

4

To hit a lofted shot from deep rough, set up the same as you would for a standard bunker shot with a wide stance and the ball in the middle (1). Open the face slightly. I keep my weight left as I turn into a virtual reverse pivot, and my right elbow slides back along my side (2). My shoulders stay level as I release the clubhead aggressively, hitting the grass two or three inches behind the ball (3). The ball will pop up just like a bunker shot. You need to swing the clubhead with speed to make sure the club cuts through the grass.

PLAYING FROM A DIVOT

If the ball is actually sitting down in the divot (instead of up on the front or back edge, where you can play a pretty conventional pitch shot up in the air if you need to), I rarely try to do more than hit a basic chip and run. If you get the bounce on the bottom of the club involved, it might kick through the divot hole crookedly and send your shot off-line. Instead, I want to dig a little bit with the leading edge of the wedge and hit a chip. It's very important to hit the ball first, and with an aggressive downward strike. If you don't lean to the left, or if you try to scoop it up out of the divot, you're going to hit it really fat and move it about a foot.

If I'm *forced* to hit something high on purpose—say there's water in front of me that I have to get over—I'm actually going to hit the ball fat on purpose. The trouble in front of you is going to get your brain screaming for you to try to lean back and help the

ball in the air. You've got to fight that, because if you lean right, you'll skull it. I'm going to aim an inch behind the ball and maintain that left tilt, so I hit down on it. I'm going to swing harder and try to fat it out of the divot like a bunker shot from really wet sand. But if I have a choice, I'm going to try to pick it out of the divot with a little chip swing.

If the ball is down in the divot, as it is here, you need to play more of a chip shot and hit the ball first.

....

LOFTED SHOT FROM AN UNEVEN LIE

You're obviously not always going to have a perfectly flat lie around the green. Subtle uphill, downhill, and sidehill lies aren't going to change the way you plan and execute a pitch shot, but you need to make some adjustments if you're forced to play a lofted shot from an uphill or downhill lie. From a downhill lie, your first choice would always be to hit something lower, along the ground. But if you do have to hit something in the air, it's crucial to keep your weight forward and your shoulders on the same tilt as the slope. What usually happens is you tilt your shoulders and spine back trying to get the ball up, which leads to fat and thin shots. I like to drop my right foot back, or closed, and kick my right knee in slightly, toward the ball, when I setup, because this helps me keep my weight left and allows me to swing back inside or on plane. Then I make sure to release the clubhead aggressively and finish with the clubhead low and moving down the slope. Remember, the ball will have a lower trajectory than normal, because the downhill slope effectively reduces the loft on your clubface.

On an uphill lie, the hill is working in your favor to help you get the ball in the air, but you have to work harder to keep your weight left. It'll actually feel like you're making a reverse pivot on your backswing, as you push yourself left against the slope of the hill. The mechanics of the shot are similar to a buried lie in the sand. I set the clubhead with my hands and wrists in the backswing and then squeeze the ball into the hill with the clubface, with a slight pivot and release of my wrists. My finish actually stops in the hillside. The slope will produce extra loft on your club, so you'll want to practice this shot to get a feel for how you need to set the clubface at address to produce the desired trajectory.

1

2

3

On a downhill lie, my shoulders match the angle of the hill, I drop my right foot back from the target line and kick my right knee in toward the ball slightly (1) to make sure my weight stays left and to give me room to swing around in the backswing. On the backswing, I aggressively cock my wrists and keep my weight left (2), then unload the club with speed through the ball (3).

1

2

3

4

The key here on this uphill flop shot is to keep my weight on my left side, even though the hill wants to push me to the right (1). To emphasize the weight staying left, I make almost a reverse pivot (2) on the backswing. Notice how my hips and shoulders stay level to the angle of the slope. I aggressively cock and uncock my wrists to produce speed on the clubhead end (3). And I make a full turn through, while my hands stay in front of my body (4).

....

CHIP FROM COLLAR

When the ball comes to rest just on shorter grass but up against the collar of longer grass, it kind of fits into the same bad-luck category of finding yourself in a divot in the middle of the fairway. If your ball was either on the short grass or the collar grass, you'd have an easy shot. But when it's actually up against the collar, it's a little trickier. I decide what shot to use based on how much of the ball I have access to and the distance to the hole. Using a putter from this lie is often the safest option, especially if at least half the ball is above the long cut of rough and there isn't too much fringe to go through before you reach the green. When making this play, you will want to swing your putter up in the backswing and then down on the ball more than you would for a normal stroke, in order to make good contact with the back of the ball.

My first choice for these shots has always been to blade my sand wedge with a putting stroke, since the bottom of my sand wedge is rounded and the clubhead easily slides through the

When the ball rests against the collar, it's easy to get a sand wedge on the back of it cleanly. You can also consider hitting this shot with your putter or playing a chip with your hybrid or fairway wood.

rough. I simply stay focused on meeting the equator or center of the ball with the leading edge of my wedge. The ball will come out rolling like a putt. If your sand wedge has a rounded leading edge, you might want to use your pitching wedge, which is straighter. Practice putting with your sand wedge on the green first, then try it with a lie against the collar.

Another popular way to play this shot is to use a hybrid or fairway wood. I still use a putting stroke with these clubs, but instead of blading the ball, like I do with a sand wedge, I hit down on the ball enough to catch it with the face of the club. These clubs are a good choice when you are farther from the hole.

BURIED LIE IN THE BUNKER

In the same way my standard bunker technique was probably a radical departure for you, my technique for getting out of a buried lie in the bunker is just as different. You want to use this method when at least two-thirds of the ball is buried beneath the sand. First, set up with a medium-width stance (feet about hip-width apart), and open your stance slightly. You need to tilt your upper body extremely left, which will put most of your weight toward the hole. Your ball position for this shot is going to be off of your left heel—which is slightly more forward than it would be for a normal bunker shot. The really unique part of the setup is that you will open the clubface dramatically and then take your grip. That runs counter to what you've probably heard about closing the face to hit from a buried lie.

Instead of angling the shaft away from the hole, like you would in my standard bunker setup, you'll have it pushed slightly toward the hole—mostly because of the steep left tilt of your body. The real objective for this shot is to simply get the ball to pop up from the buried lie and land as soft as possible. In order for impact to create this result, the swing has to be mostly up and down, instead of back and through. I set the clubhead very early in the backswing with my wrists and my elbows, keeping my hands close to my body and only turning my hips and shoulders slightly. The downswing is simply an unhinging motion of my wrists and elbows. A key element of the downswing is to keep your body leaning left and staying quiet. You really don't want to shift away from the ball on the backswing or toward the target on the downswing. Remember, the goal is to get the ball to pop up, so we're trying to create loft more than we are distance.

At impact, you're going to hit down on the ball and really dig the clubhead into the sand to pop it out. You're going to almost feel as though you're recoiling the club back after impact—it'll only travel four or five inches past the ball. Learning this recoiling feeling is critical, and it can be a challenge for players who are used to trying to help the ball out of a buried lie by scooping and lifting with the hands. I know that if you've had a lesson on hitting buried-lie shots, you probably learned to play them with a closed clubface. That's an effective way to get the ball out, but that shot will have a lot of run on it, and it's going to be tougher to control. It really only works when you have a lot of green to work with between you and the flag. I think hitting with my technique and an extremely open clubface will give you more loft and control. It's also good to go and practice, because as soon as you get the technique down, you'll see that you don't have to be as aggressive as you think. It doesn't take a big, violent swing to get the ball to pop out of that lie. Tom Pernice is an absolute master at this shot, and he's the one who showed it to me when I first came out on tour.

UNBALANCED STANCE IN THE BUNKER

If you play at a course that has facings built into the bunkers, then you know what happens when the ball is in the bunker but your feet aren't. In that situation, I bend over much more from my waist and bend my knees more. You aren't in a very stable position that way, so you have to go at the shot with more arm action than body rotation. I'm mostly trying to make good contact with the sand and simply get the ball out. If you have one foot in the bunker and one out, it's a much easier situation to have the right foot out of the bunker, since you're trying to keep your weight forward anyway. If your left foot is out, you need to exaggerate the tilt of your shoulders forward, toward the target, to compensate for your weight getting pushed back because of the unbalanced stance.

If the ball is up close to the front lip, it becomes a matter of hitting it high enough to clear it. I actually got it out of the Road Hole bunker at St. Andrews from about three feet behind the front lip. I probably had to hit that shot with 75 or 80 degrees of loft. You don't do that by laying the face open and cutting across the ball. The simplest way is to widen your stance dramatically, lower your hands and play the shaft leaned back, away from the target. The lower you get your hands, the more you increase the effective loft of the club—without making much change to your aim. I don't open my stance at all to hit it that high. I'm aimed straight at my target.

HARDPAN

A lot of players feel some anxiety about hardpan—or even a really tight lie in the fairway—because they get the feeling that the club is going to bounce into the ball. First of all, if you play the boring, basic chip shot I teach, you're going to hit the ball before you hit the ground, which removes bouncing the club into the center of the ball as a worry. Where most players get into trouble is when they lean back in an effort to create loft. You've heard from teachers that you need to lower your right shoulder to add loft to a shot. That can work with a driver, where the ball is up on a tee, because what you're really doing by tilting back is changing where the bottom of your swing is. If you move the bottom of your driver swing back an inch, you're actually putting yourself in a position to hit slightly up on the ball through impact, which is a good thing. But if you hit an inch behind a chip shot and hit up on the ball, you're going to hit some really, really bad chips. When the bottom of the swing goes back on this shot, you're dead. That's when you're bouncing the club off the hardpan and kicking the club up into the center of the ball. From hardpan, really concentrate on keeping 80 percent of your weight on your left foot and simply pivoting around your left leg. You'll get a little more backspin on this shot than on a regular chip, because there's no grass between the ball and the face of your wedge.

AND YES, THE PARKING LOT

One of the questions I get a lot about my chipping and pitching method is about whether or not using a lot of bounce makes you prone to blading shots. Well, if you don't hit the shot with good mechanics, you're going to blade some. But if you use the method I teach, you won't have any problems with blading shots. How do I know? I can take you out in the parking lot and show you how to hit pitch shots from pavement.

To hit it off pavement (or a cart path), you need to be more precise where you contact the ground. Instead of hitting behind it, you're trying to make contact with the ball and the ground at the same time. You do that by keeping your weight to the left and using a lot of wrist action to release the club. If you just try to swing the arms back and through with locked wrists, you're going to bang the bounce hard off the pavement too far behind the ball, and you'll blade it.

I actually hit about twenty shots from the parking lot at Grayhawk to get the photo you see here. I'll give you this as an ex-

treme shot, but I hit several that turned out good. It is hard on your wedge trying this one, so my main point is getting you to understand how to hit it, not how to master it.

As long as you keep your weight left and release the club, you can use a club with bounce, even off cement.

CHAPTER 8

TOUR TIPS AND TECHNIQUES

. . . .

Spend some time at a practice area during a PGA Tour event and you'll come away impressed. First of all, that commercial that says "These Guys Are Good" isn't lying. They can do some incredible things with the ball. Secondly, those guys work hard, too. The balls they hit in competition are just a fraction of the number they hit in an average week.

Practice rounds are just a small piece of what players do to prepare. It's common for a player to arrive at a tournament site on Monday night, then hit balls for an hour on Tuesday morning, spend an hour on short-game practice, play eighteen holes in a practice round, then spend another hour on the range and another hour on their short game *after* the practice round.

When you see how much talent and work goes into what these players do, it's easy to understand why I get one common question from amateur players about the work I do with world-class players. Am I teaching tour players different things—or using a different technique with them—than I am with regular players?

I'm really not. The basics and mechanics of the short game are the same for everybody, and the things that guys like Darren Clarke and Peter Jacobsen struggle with are similar to the things a 10-handicapper might have a problem with. Of course, there's a big difference in the level of expectation a tour player has compared to the average player, and in the talent level.

When a tour player comes to me for help, he wants to be as good as he can possibly be. They're almost always willing to do whatever it takes to be great—even if that means a lot of short-term "pain" in the form of extra practice. And you're obviously talking about the most capable golfers in the world—players who can do virtually whatever they want with a golf ball.

The biggest difference between teaching tour players and amateur players is the level of responsibility that goes with teaching somebody who is going to rely on what you say to earn his living. I take great pride and responsibility in all my students. I don't want any of them to have to get worse to get better. But a tour player needs to get better right now, and he can't simply hit it better seven out of ten times and call that progress. For the average player—a guy who's chunking and blading chip shots left and right—seven out of ten would be a massive improvement. For a tour player, his livelihood depends on getting it right almost ten out of ten times, under incredible pressure.

I work with tour players mostly at tournaments—with some guys making trips out to see me in Arizona once or twice a year. I'll go to twelve or fifteen events a year specifically to visit with players who are looking for my help. The guys I see for the first time at tour events fall into two categories. Some of them are in crisis, and they feel like they need to do something dramatic to solve a big problem. Other guys are looking for confirmation about what they do, or are kind of kicking the tires and learning about what I teach. We'll get together that first time and talk about what they do, and what they want to do better. Just as I would for an average player, I want to hear a tour player tell me what he thinks he's doing, so I can compare it to what I see. Some players have a great sense for what they're doing right and wrong, while others don't take a mechanical view of their swing and struggle to tell you exactly what they do or don't do. I'll explain that a tournament isn't the best place to make a change, but if the player wants to dive in and get started, we'll get to work. After that, my job isn't so much to do construction work. It's a series of visits at tournaments, where I watch the player and make sure he's where he needs to be and give him little adjustments to keep him there.

The relationship is a little different with amateur players I teach, especially if it's in a clinic situation. I want to be able to give you something to take home with you—basics that you're going to be able to apply to your game right away, and checkpoints to help you get back to where you should be. I think this book is going to serve a great purpose toward that end. It's one way to give you that feedback to stay on track. I might actually have higher expectations for your short game than you do. My goal is to get you hitting it like a tour player, while you might be satisfied with something that's less than that, but still better than where you were.

Let me use Mike Weir as an example of how I work with a tour player. We changed Mike's putting stroke slowly, over six or seven sessions. It's all headed toward the same goal—one he set for himself. That might be a statistical goal—improving where he is in the putting stats, or increasing his birdie average. But there isn't any dramatic mechanical change going on from one session to the next. We're not going from a dead stop to a full run over the space of an hour or two. When I visited Mike at tournaments, we spent some time on the practice green, but I also walked with him during practice rounds and even tournament rounds to get a sense of what he was really doing when it counted.

The Westchester event in 2006 was a good example of how my weeks out on tour usually work. I was scheduled to see Darren Clarke, but he pulled out of the tournament late. I ended up visiting a bunch of other guys on the practice range. I saw Matthias Gronberg for the first time. He soaked up a lot of information and really liked it, but decided that he wanted to really work on the changes once the season ended. I watched Doug Barron hit chips. We're buddies, and he knows that I know what he's supposed to look like in the backswing. I also spent time with Jeff Gove and Jay Delsing.

A couple of weeks later, I went to Scotland for the Scottish Open and spent time with Clarke, Paul McGinley, and Graeme McDowell. I also worked with Lee Westwood a lot. It was a lot of fun to see Lee at the Ryder Cup, having success with a method that is way closer to what I like to see than what he was doing before. Paul, for example, will tell you just what he needs. Sometimes he needs more attention—three or four hours on the putting green, trying to nail down some basics. I also walked with him six or eight holes during the tournament, at the British Masters. Other times, it might just be a checkup. He might see that I'm out and ask me if I'll take a look. He wants to know if what he's doing is consistent with the last time we talked.

Psychology is a really big part of the relationships I have with tour players. In general, a tour player is consumed with being the best. When they compare themselves to other players (and they all do), they often ask themselves if they're doing it right, or if they're doing everything they can to get better. They're heaping a lot of pressure on themselves. There's always something they're trying to protect—their playing status, their position on the money list, or a host of other things.

It's really a challenge to accept the pressure that comes with playing tournament golf and deal with the fact that you can't always play the way you know you can. For these players, the capability is very high, and the execution is also high at times. They just want to get there more often. I shot 62 on a very windy day on Sunday to come from six shots behind and win a golf tournament. You wonder where that comes from, and you want it to happen all the time. It's easy for somebody like Darren Clarke to get frustrated, because it's hard for him to get to his full capability because his capability is so high.

Does that mean that tour players are playing a different game? That you can't learn anything from what they do? Well, for most of you reading this, they *are* playing a different game when you're talking about skill level. But you *can* learn from what they do, because the fundamentals are the same. Let me take you through some of the short-game lessons I've given the tour players I work with, and you can see for yourself how similar some of the problems are. You might not be presented with the same sort of challenging situations—the pitch Peter Jacobsen hit in Hartford won him $700,000—but you should be able to see the parallels in your own game. You're going to feel pressure on the last hole of your member-guest when you've got to get up and down from the sand.

PETER JACOBSEN

Peter has one of the great full swings in the game—beautifully on-plane—and he's a fantastic ball-striker. The irony of it was that he got far away from that with his short game. When we started working together in early 2003, I immediately noticed that he had a lot more shoulder tilt in his short game than I like. He set up with his right shoulder much lower than his left, and he took the club back outside the plane with the face shut. That caused him to work the club a lot more up and down, on a verti-cal plane, than I like, rather than more around his body. That kind of upright swing puts a lot of pressure on your sense of tim-ing, because if you aren't really precise with it, you'll hit the ball fat or thin, or have to scoop at it with your hands to compensate. Whenever the club goes outside and up like that, you have to scoop. We got the club going more inside—six inches to a foot more inside—and he started hitting it with some body turn, with his shoulders a lot more level.

Once he started to do this, his short-game swing began to look a lot like the full swing he works on with Jim Hardy. This made both of us happy. He improved very quickly, to the point that he won the 2003 Greater Hartford Open as a fifty-year-old. Peter was nice enough to credit me for helping him learn the pitch shot he hit from the rough on the 15th hole on Sunday that clinched the tournament for him. He got up and down from a sketchy lie in the rough—a shot he would have had a lot more trouble hitting with his old technique.

Lately, we've been working on hitting the basic chip shot, adopting the same techniques you read about in Chapter 4. Peter's had some good success, even with a bad hip that he had to get replaced in the fall of 2006. He won the 2005 Senior Players Championship, and will continue to be a force on the Champions Tour now that he has a short game that complements his great ball-striking ability.

JAY HAAS

Sometimes even good players lose a feel and don't know where it went. Jay and I have been working together for a few years now, mostly on his putting, but also on his short game. When we first got together, he struggled hitting pitches from tight lies because he started with his weight to the right. He then shifted the grip end of the club to start the swing, and swayed off the ball. Once he felt more left at address and used more forearm rotation away on the shot instead of grip swing, he got it right away. He added a little lower-body pivot, and he started hitting those shots great.

But at the PGA in 2006, he told me he was having trouble with the generic flop shot out of the rough. As I watched him hit some shots, I realized that through impact, he was letting his arms roll over. He wasn't releasing the club early enough, and he wasn't using the bounce on the bottom of the club. The ball was coming out low and hot, and he wasn't able to consistently judge how far it was going to go. As soon as he stopped that arm rotation through the swing and kept his right palm facing up through the shot, the ball immediately started coming out softer and more consistently.

DARREN CLARKE

I first met with Darren before the PGA Championship in 2004. He was struggling with his chipping game quite a bit, and he was frustrated that he wasn't getting more out of his great ball-striking. His problem was a common one for players at all levels—he was standing too close to the ball. On a short shot, your natural impulse is to stand closer and choke down on the club, because it feels like you have more control that way. But when you get too close to it, you tend to take the backswing out and up with a closed clubface, then raise up and and out of the shot because your arms don't have room to release. That's a very steep position, and it makes for inconsistent contact.

I moved Darren farther from the ball, which immediately let him use more of his natural athletic ability to hit short-game shots. He starting swinging on a more shallow plane, with more pivot and forearm rotation. He has such great control of his trajectory on full shots, and I think the new position gave him more of that sense on his short-game shots. We spent two hours working on it, and the next day he went out and shot 65 to lead the tournament. That was very satisfying—because it showed me that he got it, and that he trusted what I had to say.

Now, we're mostly working on putting, but we spent some time in 2006 on 40- to 50-yard pitch shots. We really tightened up his shot pattern from that distance with a simple adjustment. Darren made a common good player's mistake in that he hit those shots with just arm swing and no lower-body pivot. If you get your legs involved in a small pivot, they support the upper body and really help keep the club on plane. Making that little pivot helps you control the trajectory on both low and high shots due to the added feel you gain with your hands. They're also a huge part of the rhythm of a good swing. They help you keep everything in sync. They're certainly there for more than just creating energy.

PAUL MCGINLEY

I've learned a lot from teaching Paul. He's a fantastic guy to work with because he's completely dedicated to getting better. He also helped me think more carefully about how I integrate what a player does in his full swing with what I want him to do in his short game.

Paul hits his full-swing shots with a flat to bowed left wrist. He has a lot of lag, and he really de-lofts the club at impact. That was a big part of how he played his shots around the green as well—de-lofting and hitting it low. He had definitely figured out how to manage around the green with that method of hitting it low all the time. But he saw a lot of other players playing a lot of shots with less effort by using the bounce of the club and hitting it up in the air a little more. They had shots that he didn't have.

So Paul came to me committed to becoming more versatile around the green. We worked a lot on taking the club back with some cup in the left wrist, to get some loft. To him, it really felt like he was opening the face. The other piece of the puzzle was getting him to position his weight more to the left. Before, his left shoulder came up at impact as a way to get loft on his shots. That's not the most consistent way to get that done. By moving his spine tilt left at address, he could use the bounce and the natural loft on the club. His shots became much softer and more consistent right away.

After we spent some time working on that shot, the problem that snuck in on him was adding too much loft—taking the fix too far. He had integrated the new, good backswing in with his old downswing, and the club would go right under the ball. He missed a few shots right and short. It took a while for his body to adapt to the new backswing, but as it did, he improved quickly. Now he has a softer shot to rely on from the rough around the greens and bunkers.

GRAEME MCDOWELL

Graeme is a super-talented young guy who came up through the game a lot like Paul McGinley did. Both guys played their amateur golf in the wind in Ireland. Their swings don't look alike, but they have a lot of the same characteristics—trapping the ball a lot and de-lofting the club a lot at impact. When Graeme came to the U.S. to play, he realized he needed to have a lot more variety in his shots around the green. We've spent time working on shots from long grass and the bunker, because if you can't get loft on those shots, you can't score at tour courses. The pins are just too tight to the edges of the greens.

Graeme really turns hard with his left shoulder in his full swing, and his left arm gets pulled along behind. He never really releases the club without turning his body hard. So on short shots, he wasn't able to get the bounce of the club working on the ground. We spent a lot of time getting him to set up more left, and to release the club more with his left arm and wrist independent of his shoulder movement. The feel for him was keeping his right shoulder high and back during the entire downswing. He's gotten so much better pitching the ball, and he feels more confident about being able to get up and down on tough course setups.

STEWART CINK

Stewart is a player who uses a lot of hands early in the backswing of his full swing. He did the same thing on his chip shots—and he took the club way outside and shut. Since he was picking the club up so quickly, he had to get very wristy with it to get back to impact in a decent position. We had to round his backswing out, so the club wasn't so shut. The club started coming around more square to the path, so he could release his hands properly and not scoop the clubhead.

One feel idea that really seemed to work for him was this: Your forearms have two bones in them, and if I stuck out my hand to shake yours, those bones stack on top of each other. On the backswing, you want the feeling that you're rotating those bones to the right, and the right elbow folds as it moves back along your right side. The player who is taking it back outside and shut is rotating those bones under and in the opposite direction, not to the right.

JOE DURANT

With Joe, the theme is similar to what you've heard about other players here. Sometimes what makes guys good ball-strikers hurts their short game. Joe is one of the straightest hitters of all time—he's annually among the top two or three on the PGA Tour in both driving accuracy and greens in regulation. He plays with his left wrist bowed and the club de-lofted, and with a really upright golf swing. He chipped the same way—the first move was shutting the club and lifting it. He added a lot of hinge to the right wrist, swung very steeply and let his hands get very high in the backswing. We moved him four inches farther from the ball, lowered his hands to get the shaft plane to shallow out some, and got him to rotate the club with a lot of cup in the left wrist.

DOUG TEWELL

Some players I work with don't need much, if any, modification on the technique they use. Doug is a great example of that. He hit his chips and pitches pretty well, but he never had a plan for how to practice his short game. He told me that when he went to the range to hit full shots, he always knew exactly what he was working on, and what he wanted to accomplish during that session. But he said that when he practiced his short game, he didn't know whether he was hitting good shots or bad ones, or what he should be working on to get better.

Doug loves to practice his long game, mostly because he hits it so pure. He called me to come watch his short-game practice time so I could give him some direction on how to get as much out of that time as he did when he worked on his full swing. He wanted to be able to diagnose what was going wrong with his stroke if he started to struggle out on the course. We talked about making sure he swung the club on plane, and keeping his weight left and pivoting. That was it, and he was off and running.

The other question I get a lot is about the greatest short-game shot I've ever seen. That's a hard one to answer, because there are really two components to it. You've got the actual technical difficulty of the shot and the lie, and you've got the situation in which the shot was made. I was playing in a Nike event in Mississippi, and I hit some bad shot that went off the back of the green and down the cart path. I had a building on my right and a hedge on my left, so there was nowhere to take a drop from the path. The green was elevated six feet above me, and the pin was in the back, just on the edge of the green. I ended up flopping it off the cement cart path, and it one-hopped, hit the pin, and dropped to about a foot. I would have been really happy to just get it on the green from that spot. Now, I didn't end up shooting 63, and I didn't even win the tournament. That's the greatest shot I ever hit, but it wouldn't make any great short-game shot list, because it didn't happen on the 72nd hole of a major championship.

Paul Azinger has hit two of the greatest bunker shots I've ever seen. In 1993, I watched him hole out from the bunker on 18 to beat Payne Stewart by a shot at the Memorial. He had a clump of sand behind the ball, and he had to perfectly judge how hard to swing through that sand to get the ball to clear the lip and then trickle down to the hole. It was just fantastic. The bunker shot he hit on the last hole of his singles match against Niclas Fasth at the 2002 Ryder Cup was just as good—bad lie, double break on the green—but the U.S. ended up losing the event. Still, to make a shot like that to earn a halve in a big match is clutch stuff.

Tiger Woods has an incredible short-game touch, and he also puts himself in position to win big tournaments time after time. He has plenty of good ones on his résumé, but the most incredible one is probably the chip shot he holed on the 16th green at Augusta in 2005. Chris DiMarco had hit it up there tight and was in position to make birdie, but Tiger played his chip perfectly off a huge slope and watched it break 10 feet and roll right down to the edge of the cup. Tiger has always had a flair for the dramatic, and this shot was no different. The ball teetered on the edge of the cup for what seemed like forever before it dropped in. He and his caddie, Steve Williams, went nuts, and so did the crowd. DiMarco missed his birdie putt, and Tiger ended up beating him in a playoff for his fourth green jacket.

John Daly is famous for how far he hits it, but his short-game touch deserves more attention. He has great hands, and the shot he hit to win the 2004 Buick showed them off. He was in a three-way playoff and hit his second shot on the par-5 into a bunker 30 yards from the flag. He lofted a super-high bunker shot that landed 20 feet short of the pin and trickled down to four inches. He tapped in to win for the first time on the tour since the 1995 British Open. A long bunker shot is one of the toughest in the game, and Daly had to hit his under playoff pressure, to a flag with a water hazard sitting right behind it. That was big time.

Speaking of the 1995 British Open, Daly ended up beating Costantino Rocca in a playoff, but Rocca hit three of the most remarkable short-game shots I've ever seen—all in the span of two holes. On the 17th, St. Andrews's famous Road Hole, Rocca hit his approach shot over the green and off the wall that separates the course from the town. The ball came to rest on the gravel road, in a little depression. Rocca used his putter to whack the ball out of the rut, and it trundled up onto the green to four feet, where he saved par. On the 18th, he bombed his tee shot down 30 yards from the green, then chunked the biggest pressure chip of his life, leaving his ball in the Valley of Sin. From there, he rolled in a 60-foot fringe putt to get himself into the playoff with Daly. To be able to compose yourself after making such a bad swing is pretty amazing. Daly certainly thought so. When he watched Rocca make the bomb, he looked like he was going to be sick.

Phil Mickelson's specialty is the flop shot, and he hits one that takes a tremendous amount of skill and guts. At the 2006 Memorial, he was three feet off the green in deep grass, and the flag was about 20 feet on and on a steep, downhill slope. That's a tough shot, because you've got to swing hard enough to get the club through the rough, but the shot isn't a very long one. Mickelson took a big, full flop-shot swing with his 64-degree wedge and hit the ball up in the air so that it flew about five feet and landed just on the edge of the green. It rolled down to the hole like a putt and went in for birdie. It was a much, much tougher shot than the one he hit from the rough on the 18th hole to win the PGA Championship in 2005, but the stakes were higher at Baltusrol, for sure.

Ernie Els is another guy who has underrated short-game skills. He really showed them off at the 2002 British Open, when he hit two great bunker shots on Sunday on his way to winning his first Claret Jug. The first one came on the 13th hole, where he had stuck himself right up against the sod face of a pot bunker, in a rake mark. He hit that shot basically straight up in the air to within a foot to save par. Then, on the last hole of a four-man playoff, he was stuck in another awkward lie in a greenside bunker. With one foot out of the bunker, he hit this one to five feet and made it to win the title.

Larry Mize's chip shot that won the 1987 Masters was one of the coolest to watch, because of both the situation and the imagination it took to hit it. Mize had to be considered the big underdog in his playoff with Greg Norman and Seve Ballesteros, and Norman was in prime position to win his first green jacket, with a birdie putt from the middle of the green. Mize was 15 yards short and right of the 11th green, basically needing a miracle at that point. He got one, hitting a sweet running chip that bounced up the face of the slope and rolled 50 feet into the cup for birdie. Shocked, Norman couldn't make his birdie try, and Mize won his hometown tournament. The year before, Bob Tway had holed a bunker shot on the 18th hole Sunday to beat Norman at the PGA Championship by two.

The moral of the story? If you've got a good short game, you're never out of a hole.

CHAPTER 9
SHORT-GAME DRILLS

N ow that you have all this information on short-game shots, how do you go about using it? Two ways. I'm in favor of going and experimenting with the techniques I've been talking about here. Some of it will feel different, for sure, but I'm willing to bet that you'll quickly start to feel more comfortable—and see the possibilities. The second way is to do the drills I'm going to talk about here. Even if you get the overall concept of the shots I teach, the drills will help direct you into the right positions and the right *feels* for the various short-game shots. Remember, what I'm trying to help you do is get out of the way of your natural ability. Once you try these drills a few times, it's going to feel like the short game is something that's easier to learn than you expected—not like you're opening the door to something that's complicated and is going to take a lot of maintenance to get right.

When I go out for a practice session, I like to bring a shag tube filled with balls. It's a metal cylinder with little clips on the end that you can use to pick up balls without bending over. It carries about twenty-five balls, so you can dump them out, hit them, and then go pick them up.

One important reason I use the shag tube instead of hitting a hundred balls out of the bucket is that the tube paces me. I don't just sit there mindlessly hitting balls without thinking about what I'm doing. I can hit some, then go clear the green off, then change my location and lie. Picking up my own shag balls also provides some consequences for bad shots. I've got to go run all those bad ones down, so hitting a bunch of good ones all in a little group is helpful.

If I'm going to go through a serious short-game practice session, I'll devote at least an hour to it. I'm going to be thinking seriously about technique—not just feel, like I would if I were warming up before a round. If you try some of the drills you're going to read about in this chapter, you'll be trying them in two or three cycles and seeing if they'll work for you.

I spend quite a bit of my practice time doing something that might seem boring to you—hitting simple shots out of good lies. Those are the shots you're going to face the most during a round, so it makes sense to me that you should spend the most time practicing those shots. When I watch students warming up for a session with me, I'll often see them practicing new things they're working on from a really hard lie. That's making it difficult right away, and it's hard on your confidence. Start with the basic shots from simple lies, then move on to some hard ones. You do need to practice some shots from tough lies, but keep in mind that you want to get the mechanics of your basic shots—especially if you're working on changing those mechanics—down first.

I can't stress enough that you should be moving around the practice area and varying the shots you hit. Hit some low ones, then hit some pitches, then hit some high ones. That's the secret to feel. You're learning your wedge and learning what the wedge does under different conditions. I would love to see you get to the course once a week and spend an hour just working on your short game. I believe that's a realistic schedule if you're serious about getting better. If you do that, you can improve very, very quickly. You'll see results after the first session, and after a month, you will have shaved multiple shots off your handicap.

Now that you've had a chance to experiment with these shots, let's move on to the drills.

BADMINTON

I've been trying to show the relationship between the left wrist and the clubface, and while that concept probably makes sense, it's sometimes hard to see. I like to start students out with this drill, because it reinforces that connection quickly and easily.

First, find yourself a badminton racket or something similar—a Ping-Pong paddle, tennis racket, or even a wooden spoon works just fine. Hold it with the standard short-game grip we learned. Because a racket doesn't have any loft (and it has a big head that's pretty close to you), you can immediately see what bowing and cupping the left wrist does to the face.

Your body position is similar, but when the left wrist is in a neutral position, the face of the racket doesn't have any loft of its own. When you bow your left wrist, so that the crease in the wrist folds on the underside of the arm, the face of the racket turns down, and has less loft. If you do the opposite, and cup the left wrist so that the crease forms on the top of the arm, the racket has more loft on its face.

One important point to remember about this drill—and about how your wrists should work in short-game shots—is that the face is square to the target in all of these situations. This is very different than throwing the toe end over, which would aim the racket to the left, or pulling the heel end in and opening the face, which would aim it to the right. If you bounced a ball off

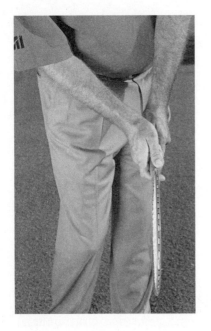

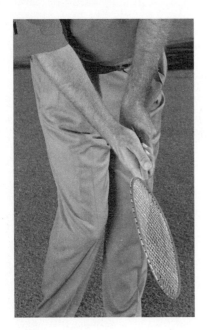

(TOP LEFT) When I hold this badminton racket, you can more clearly see the relationship between the top of the left wrist and the clubface. When the wrist is neutral, the clubface is flat, too.

(TOP RIGHT) When the left wrist is bowed toward the target, the face of the badminton racket is angled more toward the ground (or de-lofted), not aimed to the left.

(BOTTOM LEFT) When the left wrist is cupped, the face of the racket has added loft. You can do this without changing the aim.

the face of the racket in any of these three positions, it would go straight at the target. Only the loft on the ball would be different, and that's what we're going for here.

ONE-FOOT PIVOT

You've heard me say over and over again that the weight needs to stay left on your short-game shots, and you need to make a level pivot as opposed to tilting back or sliding. To really get a sense of what it feels like to make that kind of pivot, try this simple drill. At address, put all of your weight on your left foot and move your right foot back so that only your toe is on the ground. Hold the club in your left hand and balance yourself with it out in front of you. Now, simply turn your right hip back, keeping your shoulders and hips level. Since you don't have any place to move your weight back or tilt back away from the ball, you're forced to stay level. Keep your weight on your left leg, then turn back and through. You're trying to keep the left side of your belt from raising above the right side as you turn through the shot. Do this a few times and you're immediately going to get a good sensation of rotary action on top of a single axis, not a slide or a tilt. We're standing on two feet and using two arms, which makes it hard to keep a single axis. But since we're dealing with such small shots in the short game, you want to simplify it to one axis—the left leg. That's what we're accentuating here.

1

2

3

To feel a level hip turn, stand on your left foot and balance yourself with your club (1). Then, turn back with the right hip (2). If you tilt back, you'll lose your balance and fall. Turn through the shot and balance on your left foot (3), keeping the belt line square.

....

THROW AND RELEASE

On a pitch shot, the clubhead end of the club releases through impact. This is what gives you clubhead speed and loft on the shot. To get the sensation of release, hold the club in your right hand (holding it at the bottom of the grip) at waist height and swing it back, letting the weight of the clubhead pull your wrist into a cocked position. Your right palm and the clubface will be pointing at the sky. The shaft will be parallel to the ground, and hinged at a right angle to your body. I want you to now release the clubhead with your wrist, like you are driving a nail into the wall with the heel of the club. Your palm stays facing up, and the end of the grip hinges under your forearm. I do not want you to roll your forearm any on this drill. Feel the clubhead hinge back and release through almost on its own, without any pull on the grip.

ELBOWS

Once you feel the cocking and uncocking, build on that with this drill, which will help you learn what the elbows should do during a pitch swing. Start by holding the club in your left hand, extending it out waist high toward the target. Let it swing freely across you body, so that your left arm is resting against your stomach and the club is pointing parallel to the target line and away from the target. Holding this position, slide your right hand into place on the grip. One thing you'll notice right away is how far to your side the right elbow is. For most people, this is a dramatic change—the elbow will be folded much more along your side and behind you than before. From this position, you can make a simple swing from the inside with some body turn and hit it solid every time. That's the feel we're trying to develop here.

After you've done the drill with your right hand a few times, switch the club to your right hand to start. Extend the club out along the target line, pointing away from the target. Swing your right arm freely across until it rests along your stomach. Then, put your left hand on the handle. Feel how similar this left elbow position is to the right elbow position in the first part of this drill. I teach less arm and grip swing for short-game shots than most players are used to. What this drill helps you learn is how to allow the clubhead to swing freely through the proper use of the elbow hinging back and through the shot.

Notice how your hands stay centered in your chest when you swing this way, from the time you swing back to the time you finish. If you feel your hands moving away from the center of your chest, it means you're pushing and pulling the grip out of place. Watch almost any tour player hit a pitch shot and you'll see him finish with his hands in the center of his chest, pulled in pretty close.

SEQUENCING

One of the common mistakes I see players make when trying to pivot is to turn only the upper body through, leaving the lower body stationary. If this is your tendency, you will bring the club down to the ball from an outside path, or over the top. Try this drill to get a feel for how the lower body should move in a short-game swing.

Hold the club out in front of you waist high, with your standard grip. Start by turning your hips and shoulders to the right.

Supporting the club with one hand helps you feel what the elbows should do during a pitch swing. Start with the club extended toward the target in your left hand (1). Let the clubhead swing freely across your body, to where your forearm is up against your stomach (2). Hold this position, then put your right hand on the club (3), so you can feel where your right elbow should be. It will probably feel more behind you than you expect. With the right hand, start with the club extended back from the target (4), and perform the drill the opposite way to get a feel for the left elbow after impact (5, 6).

Now, feel like your body has been split in half at the belly button. Start by turning your knees and hips back toward the target, but maintain your shoulders, upper body, and club in the turned-back position.

Because your upper and lower body *are* actually connected, when you turn your knees and hips toward the target, that movement will eventually pull your upper body around toward the target as well. Make some practice swings retaining your upper body in the turned-back position until it gets pulled back around by your leg action. You can even exaggerate the move by making some slightly bigger swings to get the feel of it.

When you actually hit a chip or pitch shot, this is the kind of movement you want—the lower body leading and pulling the upper body along. A chip shot is turned through almost entirely by a pivot, while a pitch shot requires more release of the clubhead through impact. This drill will also help you with your full swing, because this creation of torque and coil between your upper and lower body is what creates power.

PITCHING LADDER

I like to use this drill on the practice range to dial in my pitching distance control. Start by pitching a ball out there about 30 yards. It will land and then roll out a little bit. Hit the next shot, but have it land where the first ball came to rest. That ball will then roll out a little bit past the first ball. Repeat that with the next shot and the next, with the goal of landing each shot where the previous one came to rest. This obviously helps your distance control, and it works great on helping direction, too. When you're done, you should have a neat, straight line of balls out to about 60 yards away. I like to pick a flag as the ultimate target, then work my way in steps out to the flag. As you get better, you can try to put more and more balls into the "ladder," both by being really precise in where you land your shots and by hitting shots with more loft.

SAND PRACTICE STATION

Before we get to any actual swing drills from the bunker, here's something you can do every time you practice from the sand— even when you're warming up before a round. I draw a line along my toe line, square to the target, and then draw a half-moon shape around the ball, from the outside of my left foot to the outside of my right foot. Then, I draw a T-line connected to the half-moon line to show my ball position—which is slightly ahead of center. This reminds me of all the setup and swing alignments I need. I aim myself square to the target line (not open to it). The club comes back and around me (not up and out). The club comes around me and through impact, and then around me again on the through swing (not pushed out down the target line). The T-line also reminds me of where my ball position should be—two to three inches in front of center.

SWING NARROW IN THE SAND

I use the term "narrow" a lot when I'm describing a sand shot. This drill will definitely help you get a sense for just what that feels like—as opposed to a wide position with the hands extending away from the body. Start out in the standard address position in the bunker, with your feet set apart at shoulder width, and the ball just forward of center. Then, pull the club up to your chest, with your arms pulled back to your sides and the grip pulled toward your belly button. If you have a hat on, the shaft of the club will hit the brim. Keeping your weight firmly on your left side, turn your hips away from the ball, keeping your arms folded and the club close to your chest. This is what's known as a narrow swing. It's the opposite of reaching away with your arms on the backswing and letting the grip extend out in front of you.

Keep your arms pulled close to you, then pivot through as a reaction to your arm swing, which is a different pivot sequence than most of our other short shots. Throw the clubhead end of the club at the sand with the wrists and arms while keeping your

To feel how narrow a good bunker swing is, start by retracting the club up to the middle of your chest (1), pulling your arms close to your body. Then, make a full shoulder turn back (2), keeping your weight mostly on your left foot. Then, use your wrists to swing your clubhead down on the sand behind the ball (3).

right shoulder high and back. Your hips should turn only after the ball is gone. It's going to feel like you're casting the club—and that's a move that's pretty much unique to this shot. If you simply turn and cast the club, uncocking your wrists as fast as you can on the downswing, you'll be exposing the bounce on the bottom of the wedge. You'll start effortlessly splashing sand—and getting the ball out of the bunker. When you get the feel for this, you'll instantly hear a different noise when you hit a good shot. It's more of a hollow, thumping sound.

ONE HAND IN THE SAND

Another way to get the feel for how the wrists cock and uncock on a bunker shot is to practice hitting the sand with one hand. If you have ever used a hammer to drive a nail, you have used your wrist in an up-and-down movement. If you turn your arm and the club to an on-plane position and then use the same release as the hammering motion, you're on your way to better bunker shots. The key to the proper feel is that when you release the club, you want the bounce edge of your sand wedge to contact the sand first. As the club swings past impact, your right palm needs to face up toward the sky. A big problem people have is that when they release the clubhead, they roll the club over, which de-lofts the face and has the bounce on the club facing up, not toward the sand.

Don't jump into the bunker and immediately start trying to hit full bunker shots with just your right hand. Start small and feel your wrist load and unload. Don't take the club back any higher than your knees, and practice simply splashing some sand out with the one hand. I make sure to hold the club very lightly. If you get too tight on the grip, you're going to restrict how your wrist can bend, and the swing will get very stiff and awkward.

Once you get a feel for splashing the sand, grow it by adding some arm swing to it. Once you've learned how to load and unload the right wrist this way, it's simply a matter of putting your left hand on the club and copying the move you just made.

You can try to hit the ball with this drill, but it does take some strength to relase the club fast enough with one hand to play a shot. I'll sometimes start out a bunker clinic doing it, just to get the students' attention. Most of the time, average players are so intimidated by a basic bunker shot that they can't even imagine hitting one with one hand. But by the end of one practice session—using this drill and the one right before it—they're hitting it out with one hand themselves.

Making a bunker swing with one hand forces you to load your wrists completely (1) on the backswing, then unload them (2) to hit the ball. Hit the ball with your wrist action, not by pulling with your arm.

You will get the greatest benefit using these drills during your practice time, but they can also be helpful to create feel in a warm-up session before a round. Before a tournament round, I always go right from the locker room to the practice green. I'll spend ten minutes there hitting some nice, easy putts to get some feel in my hands. I want to see what my stroke feels like, and to get a feel for what the green is doing in terms of speed.

After that, I'll go to the range. I work my way through my bag, starting with my shortest clubs, for about thirty minutes. If the chipping area is relatively close, I'll go there next and hit a dozen sand shots. My only thought on those is to get a sense for what the sand is like—what the consistency is. Is it wet or dry? Will my ball tend to stay up on top of it or settle down in the sand a little bit? I'm programming my brain for the feel. My bunker play is about letting my hands work and releasing the club. It's a different swing than hitting a standard shot.

The practice putting green is usually near the first hole, so I'll head there last, fifteen to twenty minutes before my actual tee time. I'll take my 58-degree wedge and hit some small chip shots. I want to feel the ground, and how firm or soft it is under the grass. I want to feel the bounce on my club, and feel how the club is responding in the grass and in the rough.

Your warm-up session for a round isn't the best time to be concerned about technique, but what I hope you're taking away from this book is self-awareness of your short-game tendencies. If you are struggling with getting the feel you want for a chip, pitch, or sand shot, a few swings using one of these drills may just set you straight for a good day. Five minutes before I go to the tee, I get my putter out and hit some short ones. It is a simple habit of seeing the ball go into the hole before I go out and play.

The next time you play, think of your pre-round time as a way to get loose, find your rhythm and tempo, and get a sense of feel for the day, not as a time to make some changes in your mechanics. Hit the bare minimum number of full shots it takes to get loose and get some feel for your long clubs, then devote most of your time to chipping and putting. Feeling more touch on and around the greens is going to do a lot more for your score than anything you're going to be able to find for your full swing thirty minutes before you play. And I'm not just saying that because I teach the short game.

Watch what Tiger Woods does before a tournament round and you'll see he follows that kind of schedule. He's warming up beforehand, not practicing. The serious work on his full swing comes when he's finished. I've seen him close the range down past dark on a night after a tournament round at a major championship when he wasn't happy with something in his game. Post-round practice is also good because the things you struggled with are still fresh in your mind.

CHAPTER 10

SHORT-GAME QUICK REFERENCE GUIDE

. . . .

I'm sure all of this short-game information has been a lot for you to digest. Anytime you decide to make changes to your game—whether it's your putting stroke, full swing, or short game—it's going to cause some anxiety. The first piece of hitting good shots is understanding your new technique and feeling comfortable with what you're doing. Doing something differently is going to take you out of your comfort zone in the beginning. But if you spend some time at the short-game practice area and try the drills from the last chapter, I promise you're going to see positive results.

Does that mean you're never going to struggle? Absolutely not. I visit every tour player I work with on a regular basis for "checkups," to make sure they're still doing what they want to be doing with their putting and short game. Everybody—myself included—gets out of whack in terms of fundamentals every once in a while. This quick reference guide will essentially be an extra set of eyes on your short game, and help you get back on track if you run into problems.

BASICS

- I define a chip shot as a shot that is played with a de-lofted clubface position. I'm hitting the ball first and making contact with the ground with the leading edge of the clubface out in front of the ball. A pitch shot uses more wrist action, and I'm making contact with the ground with the bounce on the bottom of the club.

- Grip the club so that it runs down in your fingers, not up across the palms. Gripping it in the palms restricts the wrist action you need to be able to control the clubface in a wide variety of shots.

- A neutral grip is the best for short-game shots. The V's created by your thumbs and the sides of your hands should be parallel to each other and pointing to your right collarbone, not your chin (weak) or your right shoulder (strong).

- If your grip is too strong, you're starting with your forearms already rotated, and you'll hit shots low and to the left unless you hold off your release. If your grip is too weak, you'll struggle to release the club properly and tend to flip your wrist, which opens the face and scoops the ball.

- Tension is the biggest short-game killer. If you tighten the muscles in your arms and hands, you won't be able to swing smoothly, or have any feel or touch.

- For chips and pitches, a narrower stance is good, because it promotes a pivot instead of a slide back and forth. My feet range from inside hip-width apart for a long pitch to three or four inches apart for a small chip.

THIS IS YOUR RECEIPT AND IS NOT A TICKET FOR TRAVEL

...rget, so that if you drew a line in front ... parallel to the target line (the line ... here you're trying to hit it). A line in ... hips, and knees should also be square

...ou should have sixty-five percent of ... foot, and keep it there during the ... ight and tilt toward the target will ... he shot level and swing the club on a ... pact. If the shoulders tilt back and ... right, you'll tend to hit behind the

...move the ball back in your stance. That's been taught as a way to ensure making a downward strike on the ball, but it causes a disastrous shoulder tilt to the right. Play the ball in the middle of your stance and keep your weight left.

• The position of the left wrist controls the trajectory of your shots. If the wrist is bowed at impact (so that the creases on the wrist appear on the bottom), you'll hit it low. If the wrist is neutral, you'll hit a mid-height shot. If the wrist is cupped (so that the creases are on the top, where your watch face would be), you'll hit it high. The wrist should be bowed on a chip, neutral on a pitch, and cupped on a bunker shot or flop shot.

CHIPPING STROKE

- The chipping stroke is a very small version of the bottom of a real swing.

- Stand taller to the ball than you would for a full shot, with your elbows hanging soft, not hyperextended under your shoulders.

- The grip end of the club doesn't move very much. Your right elbow folds around your right side, which allows the club-head to swing back. You're pivoting around your left side, and the right elbow unfolds through impact, with the left elbow folding similarly after impact.

- Your hands lead the clubhead through impact, which creates lag. The club should hit the ball first, and then the ground, on a descending blow. You keep pivoting through impact, and the hands end up low and square to the center of your chest at finish.

- The wrists hinge slightly in the takeaway, and then remain hinged through and after impact as a result of your bowed left wrist.

COMMON CHIPPING PROBLEMS

- If you're working on the rotation and pivot, you might be off in your timing. The sequence needs to work from the ground up. If you turn the upper body back through the ball first, before the lower body, you'll swing over the top and from the outside. Your arms swing in the direction that the shoulders point, so if you turn the shoulders too early, they'll point to the left at impact. You can diagnose this by where you're making contact with the ball on the clubface. If you're swinging from outside in, you'll hit it off the toe. Your goal is to move those little grass marks more to the center of the club. I actually wear out a little circle on the face of my wedge toward the heel side of center.

- Players sometimes try to de-loft the club, so they set up with the hands pressed forward, toward the target. You need a slight amount of forward press at address, but the de-lofting of the club should come from your transition, not from how you set your hands.

- People who have the ball too far forward often do so because the left foot is flared out, and it's harder to see. It feels like the ball is in the right spot, but it's actually forward. Turn your toe 90 degrees to the target line and set your ball position first, then angle your toe out if you need to.

- If you try to pivot, but are really sliding, you're going to hit the ball thin and fat. When the left hip moves forward, the right shoulder goes down and the head goes behind the ball. You're tilting in the wrong direction.

PITCHING STROKE

- A pitch is essentially a grown version of the chip, with more wrist action back and through.

- The main difference here is that you set up with the shaft more neutral than you would on a chip shot. On a chip, the hands are pressed more forward, toward the target. On a pitch, the shaft is in a more neutral, straight-up-and-down position. This exposes more of the bounce to the ground.

- The turn and pivot on a pitch are the same as a chip, just sequenced slightly differently. As you bring the club back, you're actively setting the wrists and hands, then unhinging your wrists through impact. The pivot leads the club in the chip, and moves along evenly with the club on a chip.

- A good wrist hinge feels like the same movement you'd hammer a nail with—the release through is on the same tilt as the shaft plane. Through impact your right palm will face up.

- Like the chip shot, the clubhead end should be moving much more than the grip end. Concentrate on making a smaller arm swing with more wrist cock, not a large arm swing.

COMMON PITCHING PROBLEMS

- To hit a good pitch, the clubhead has to be moving faster than the grip end. If you move the grip end too much, pulling on it to speed the head up, you're only slowing the whole club down.

- Players often set up with the right shoulder lower than the left, to try to help the ball in the air by scooping it. This actually makes the shot harder, because it makes the low point of the swing very inconsistent. Keep your weight to the left and focus on keeping the shoulders level through the swing.

- Sometimes players feel like they should swing in to out, so they swing up and out through impact. The hands get high and cross the target line, which causes the ball to push out to the right. The club bottoms out too soon, as well, and you sometimes get fat shots. Through impact, your hands should finish around you, low and to the left.

- It's common to see players aimed too far to the left, because they're used to opening the clubface and cutting across the ball. A squarer stance will help you swing the club around your body both back and through, which will help your shots fly straight with square backspin, not sidespin.

SAND SHOT STROKE

- You've probably been taught to open your stance way up, play the ball forward, and open the clubface at setup. I don't advocate that method.

- I like you to take a wide, square stance, with the ball just forward of middle and the clubface only slightly open. Your stance should be wider than shoulder width, and you should bend your knees as though you're squatting to sit in a low chair. Your hands will feel as though they're set very low.

- Like the chip and pitch, you need to set your weight and spine tilt firmly on your left side. In the swing, your hands stay close to your body and your arms are pulled in, not extended. Keep the weight left, and slap the sand with the back of your wedge one to three inches behind the ball.

- Make a conscious effort to turn your hips in the backswing but remember to always stay in your left spine tilt. This will seem as though you are reverse pivoting, but it will help keep you from tilting back on the downswing, which causes fat shots and skulls.

- The angle of the shaft at address should be slightly away from the target, which means the clubhead is slightly ahead of the hands. This, coupled with the hands set low at address, increases the effective loft of the club.

COMMON BUNKER PROBLEMS

- The biggest mistake I see is playing the ball too far forward. That forces you to tilt back to reach, which is a death move out of the bunker.

- This shot requires a free swing of the clubhead, but not a big arm swing. I see a lot of big arm swings, with players flailing at the ball. The relationship between actually letting the club cast and release with the hands is sometimes hard to get, because players tend to pull hard with the arms and body to hit the shot. Your downswing should start with the release of the clubhead by the hands and arms, while keeping your back turned closed and your spine in a left tilt as long as possible. Your body turns through as a consequence of the club going by. It doesn't lead with the club following.

- Sometimes players who try to release the club like I teach end up actually rolling the club over and get the toe pointing down. They release, but they also cross the forearms. You need to release but keep the clubface facing up. Don't swing your arms as much, but slap the sand with the back of the club. You should feel your right palm facing up in the air through impact.

CHOOSING YOUR SHOT

- First, diagnose the obstacles in front of you. Do you have to carry a hazard or a bunker? Do you need to carry a shot up onto a tier, or down to a lower level on the green?

- Read the conditions. Is there grain on the green? Is the green firm and fast, or damp and slow? What is the overall break on the green, and what will it do to your shot?

- The shot you pick depends on these factors, plus your comfort level with the situation. If you're under pressure and don't need to make a par, it's sometimes better to play a lower-risk shot more toward the middle of the green, rather than flying something back to the pin.

- Be specific about where you want your shot to land (I am for a basketball hoop–sized spot), and judge how hard to play the shot to that spot instead of focusing on the flag. Being too concerned about the flag can lead you to make a big backswing and decelerate through impact.

- In your practice stroke, visualize your shot landing on the spot you picked, then step up and hit the real shot before that image dissolves in your head.

EQUIPMENT

- The three main characteristics of your short-game clubs are loft, bounce, and lie angle.

- Loft is the measure of how high and far a club will hit the ball. A club with more loft, like a 58- to 60-degree wedge, will hit the ball higher and shorter than a 20-degree 3-iron.

- Bounce angle is the amount of material that hangs below the leading edge of the wedge. Like loft, it's measured in degrees. Most lofted wedges range from 3 degrees of bounce (not very much) to 16 degrees (a big flange).

- Lie angle is how upright or flat the clubhead is built in relation to the shaft. The closer you stand to the ball, either because of your setup or because of your build, the more upright the club should be. In general, I think wedges should be built with a slightly flatter lie angle than standard (62 degrees instead of 64), because I teach a flatter short-game swing.

- The goal is to have a collection of wedges that covers the variety of full and short shots you need to hit.

- I use a 58-degree wedge with 12 degrees of bounce, a 52-degree gap wedge with 8 degrees of bounce and a 48-degree pitching wedge. I chose the gaps between my wedges based on how far I hit each club from the fairway.

- I hit virtually all my short-game shots with my 58-degree wedge. I believe it's easier to learn how to adapt one club to a variety of different shots than judging distance with a lot of different clubs.

- The playing characteristics of wedges are easy to change. Clubfitters can easily bend a wedge to give it more or less loft, or a more upright or flatter lie angle. I even had some of the bounce shaved off the heel of my 58-degree wedge so I can lay the club flatter on the ground from tight lies if I need to.

TROUBLE SHOTS

- The shot you hit from various situations is completely dependent on the lie you have. If you can get the club on the back of the ball cleanly, you can play a standard chip or pitch shot.

- From deep rough, when you can't contact the back of the ball cleanly, you can play a version of the standard bunker shot. Widen your stance and lower your hands to increase the effective loft of the club. Then make a narrow turn, keeping your hands closer to your body. Release the club aggressively and hit two or three inches behind the ball to pop it up out of the grass. Remember to keep the face of the club pointing up. Don't let it turn over in the grass, or you'll smother the shot.

- On uneven lies, the first priority is to maintain your balance and your weight to the left, toward the target. This is easier to do, obviously, from a downhill lie than an uphill one.

- When your ball comes to rest against the collar, you can either play a bladed wedge shot (risky), or use your putter or hybrid club (safer). The bladed wedge is a nice shot because it puts some topspin on the ball, which makes it roll out like a putt right away. The ball will pop up on you more when you hit it with a putter or hybrid, but the flat soles of those clubs will glide through the collar grass, giving you more margin for error.

- From a buried lie in the bunker (more than two-thirds of the ball below the surface of the sand), open the clubface 60 to 70 degrees at setup and get into in a wide stance. Tilt your shoulders dramatically to the left and play the ball slightly more forward in your stance than a standard bunker shot. Keep your weight and tilt left on the backswing. You need to set the club up steeply with your hands and wrists, then aggressively release the club down and into the sand, one inch behind the crater your ball is setting in. Keep the clubface open through impact and the ball will pop up out of the sand and land relatively softly.

- To hoist the ball up high and quickly out of the bunker, take your standard bunker stance, but move farther from the ball and lower your hands more. This increases the loft of the club. Tilt more to the left at address and make sure to keep your right palm facing up when you release through the ball.

ACKNOWLEDGMENTS

After enjoying the work that went into *The Art of Putting* so much, I was really looking forward to putting together *The Art of the Short Game* and giving players everywhere a complete idea of how I think about shots from 50 yards in. I wasn't disappointed, and we had a lot fun in the process, too—even when the temperature got over 110 in Scottsdale. The team of *Golf Digest* guys I work with were great again—Matthew Rudy on the words and J. D. Cuban on the photographs. Scott Waxman got us a great deal, and Patrick Mulligan at Gotham Books did a nice job of editing the book.

I want to say thanks to my dad, Frank Utley, who became a golf fanatic when I was ten years old. He was my first coach, and he taught me how to think, both on the golf course and off. My mom, Ruby, taught me patience and positive thinking. My brother John has been a best friend forever and is now the ultimate business associate.

Ken Lanning has been the most dominant figure in my golf life. The more I learn over the years, the more I realize that the things Mr. Lanning told me when I was a teenager were right. Along that line, Jim Parkin, from Poplar Bluff, Missouri, sat me down and explained the short game to me—things I'm using and teaching to this day. Rich Poe gave me a golf scholarship at the University of Missouri, and was a great mentor and friend. While I was at Missouri, an assistant pro named Brian Allen showed me a lot of cool shots around the practice green at the Country Club of Missouri. He probably doesn't know it, but he had a big impact on me turning into the player I've become.

Craig Harrison was the first teacher I had after school, and he was there for my first PGA Tour win. He really pushed me to work hard, and I owe him a lot for that. Other teachers who have been positive influences on me are Fred Griffin, Rob Akins and Jim Hardy.

Ed Roberson took a big risk on a young pro, sponsoring me when nobody else was knocking down my door. His support gave me the ability to make some choices at the start of my career. Buddy Henry gave me a sponsor's exemption into his PGA Tour event in Chattanooga. I won that week, and it changed my life.

I would like to mention Dillard Pruitt, Fred Wadsworth, and Brandel Chamblee as well. Those guys were my running buddies when I turned pro. We traveled the mini-tours together, played practice rounds together, ate a ton of bad food, and slept in a lot of lousy hotel rooms. We'll always be lifelong friends.

I owe Tom Pernice a debt of gratitude, for sure. He showed me a better way to hit a bunker shot, and a lot of the other shots I know around the green. It's been great to see him have success on the PGA Tour after working so hard at it for so long. He's been a great friend.

I have to thank my wife, Elayna, more than anyone. She's been my partner, my wife, my coach, and my best friend. I certainly couldn't have had the career I've had without her help.

I also want to acknowledge my Lord and Savior—the giver of great gifts, who has given me the passion to encourage others not just to know Him, but to know and understand golf a little bit better.